BLACKBEARD
and Other Pirates
of the Atlantic Coast

ALSO BY NANCY ROBERTS

America's Most Haunted Places
Civil War Ghost Stories and Legends
Ghosts and Specters
Ghosts of the Southern Mountains and Appalachia
Haunted Houses
North Carolina Ghosts & Legends
South Carolina Ghosts from the Coast to the Mountains
Southern Ghosts
The Gold Seekers
This Haunted Southland
Ghosts of the Carolinas

BLACKBEARD

and Other Pirates
of the Atlantic Coast

Nancy Roberts

 JOHN F. BLAIR, PUBLISHER   WINSTON-SALEM, NORTH CAROLINA

BOOK DESIGN BY DEBRA LONG HAMPTON
PRINTED AND BOUND BY R. R. DONNELLEY & SONS

Grateful acknowledgment is made
to Suzanne Tate of Nags Head Art
for the use of Edward Powell's painting,
Blackbeard at Teach's Hole
for the jacket illustration.

Library of Congress Cataloging-in-Publication Data

Roberts, Nancy, 1924–
    Blackbeard and other pirates of the Atlantic coast /
Nancy Roberts.
        p.   cm.
    Includes bibliographical references.
    ISBN 0-89587-098-3   :
    1. Pirates—Atlantic Coast (U.S.)—History. 2.
Atlantic Coast (U.S.)—History, Naval. I. Title.
II. Title: Blackbeard.
F106.R74   1993
975' .00946—dc20   93–698

Contents

Preface

One event invariably leads to another, and for me this book really occurred because of a series of ghost stories I wrote for the *Charlotte Observer*. Carl Sandburg read them, and at his suggestion, they were published as my first book. That book is now entitled *North Carolina Ghosts & Legends*. Successive books and collections of stories about the supernatural inspired companion filmstrips.

One day a librarian asked, "Nancy, have you ever thought of doing a filmstrip about pirates?"

It's hard for me to resist challenges, and a filmstrip entitled *Blackbeard and Other Pirates* became my next project. I might have known it would work the other way around, too, and I would hear, "Have you thought of doing a book about pirates?"

Yes, I did think about it, but I was always too busy doing the next book, whether it was *America's Most Haunted Places*, *The Gold Seekers* or, most recently, *Civil War Ghost Stories and Legends*.

Nevertheless, my desire for more information about the pirates' lives, which I developed as I worked on the pirate filmstrip, finally compelled me to write this book. No longer need I resist my fascination with pirates. Now all the memories of childhood returned to me like waves surging in from the sea—weeks spent with my parents at Ocracoke, North Carolina, listening for hours to stories about Edward Teach, the infamous "Blackbeard"; walking along a sandy shore after a storm wondering if I might find a gold doubloon; or sometimes just sitting and staring out over the water at the place called "Teach's Hole" where Blackbeard anchored his ship.

Somewhere beneath the waters off the Outer Banks still lies the wreck of the ship on which the notorious pirate fought his last gory battle with Lieutenant Maynard, and near it may lie that herculean frame of Blackbeard—a skeleton without a head! And the head itself? Was it really taken to Virginia and made into a gruesome cup which the owner flaunted to watch his guests shiver in horror?

Later I discovered that Blackbeard once roamed, not just the Outer Banks of Carolina, but the entire Atlantic coast from Maine south. Other pirates of almost equal interest were the cruel, perhaps even insane, Charles Vane; New England's bestial Charles Gibbs; the rakish Captain "Calico Jack" Rackham; the independently wealthy gentleman pirate, Stede Bonnet; Captain Thomas Tew, who built a fine house at Newport, Rhode Island, and might be called one of the first socialites of the area; the colorful pirate orator, Samuel Bellamy; Captain William Kidd, whose name became synonymous with terror; and Boston's John Quelch, who went to the noose still convinced that "the system was unfair" to men "who only wanted to bring in treasure to improve the economy." And then there were the women pirates—brutal, courageous, callous figures like Rachel Wall and Mary Read, or the red-headed Anne Bonny who was known for her beauty as well as her fighting ability.

This book is not intended to take the place of an academic treatise, but I have spent weeks researching at the Library of Congress, making phone calls to libraries eliciting their cooperation, and visiting cities or islands frequented by pirates the length of the Atlantic coast from Portland, Maine; Portsmouth, New Hampshire; Boston, Massachusetts; and Provincetown, Massachusetts, on Cape Cod—where the relics of Samuel Bellamy's *Whydah* are on display—to such well-known pirate haunts as Beaufort, Bath and Ocracoke, North Carolina, as well as Charleston, South Carolina, and St. Augustine, Florida.

I am most grateful not only for the cooperation of libraries, but for historical societies and individuals. Thanks are also due my husband, Jim Brown, who participated in some of the research and was wonderfully tolerant during my periods of occasional frustration.

The stories in this book are designed to draw the most authentic pictures possible of the adventurers who lived such dangerous, violent lives. Quotes of what was actually said, as they have come down to us, have been merged with conversations one can imagine taking place to link the historic events in these people's lives.

May you find these men and women pirates as fascinating as I have!

Nancy Roberts

Introduction

This introduction has been written for those who would like additional background information about piracy and its history. You may read it before the stories, or you may find it of even more interest after reading them.

During the seventeenth and early eighteenth centuries, 2,000 or more buccaneers harassed the Atlantic coast from Maine to Florida.

Charleston, Philadelphia, New York and other ports were early pirate havens, and the Pennsylvania and Maryland waterfronts were familiar to the likes of "Blackbeard" (Edward Teach) and the notorious Charles Vane. Chesapeake Bay was so pirate-infested that Virginia's Governor Nicholson sailed out to fight them himself.

In Annapolis, Maryland, and Williamsburg, Virginia, pirate "gentlemen" dealt regularly with local silversmiths who stored their treasure while the pirates were "out on account"—their term for their profession.

Stolen cargo was brought into port and sold with the help of greedy merchants eager for high profits. Public officials such as Governor Charles Eden of North Carolina, dishonest port officials and tradesmen made piracy a profitable livelihood. Savannah, Georgia; Charleston, South Carolina; Edenton, North Carolina; and, of course, the puritanical Boston, Massachusetts, and Providence, Rhode Island, were all ports that welcomed pirates.

During the seventeenth and eighteenth century—and long before—pirates came from every part of the world and often hunted their prey thousands of miles from their home base. Spanish treasure fleets laden with gold and luxuries, sailing from the New World or the West Indies back to Europe, attracted pirates from all over the world, and by the mid-seventeenth century they had formed a pirate confederacy, "The Brothers of the Coast." Members were English, Spanish, French, Dutch, Portuguese, Indian and African.

The Golden Age of Piracy—which historian Hugh E. Rankin dates from 1689 to 1718—actually occurred because of the English Parliament's unpopular trade laws that encouraged smuggling in cheaper goods on which no duties had been paid and no questions asked. By the end of the seventeenth century a pirate ship route was operating regularly out of New England. It was manned by a company of seamen, paid, outfitted and armed by wealthy merchants to go to the Far East, plunder the ships of native traders and scurry back with luxury goods to sell in the colonies.

There had always been the question of who was a pirate and who was a privateer. Spain, England, France and Holland warred with one another so frequently during the seventeenth century that the line between a privateer and a pirate could change with the flourish of a pen on a treaty. A privateersman received a "letter of marque" from his government, which was a permission to attack the enemy in wartime. In some instances news of peace might be late in arriving and a ship captain, unaware that his country was suddenly at peace, would unintentionally commit piracy when he attacked and plundered another vessel. When such cases were tried by the courts, it was not always easy to be sure whether the captain knew of the treaty. If so he had committed a serious crime.

The moment a captain seized the ship of a nation with whom his country was at peace, he automatically crossed the line from privateering to piracy. And many former privateers did just that.

Unfortunately, there were many occasions when, somewhere out in the vastness of the open sea, a ship whose crew had turned pirate intentionally attacked the ship of a friendly nation. And after all, who was there to see and report the crime? For seamen—always poorly paid—piracy was a strong temptation. And for those who had once experienced the fabulous riches from wartime privateering, it could be even harder to resist.

Governments and merchants did not take a stand against the immorality of piracy until it began to cost them money. Only when pirates captured vessels carrying commercial cargo in which wealthy men held a financial interest was there a public outcry against piracy and a demand that pirates be caught. Once considered profitable to deal with, pirates eventually came to be hated.

We tend to believe that people back in those days were very isolated from news of world events, but that was not as true as we might think. News traveled amazingly fast. One ship would talk across the water to a passing vessel through megaphones, or ships might sail along together for a day or two. The sea could be a lonely place, and conversation and the exchange of news from various ports relieved the monotony. Ship masters and officers would make friendly visits back and forth at sea or while anchored in port. Bars were also rife with gossip. Seamen from different countries, including those from pirate ships, drank and caroused together while information was often carelessly exchanged.

But to return to the subject of piracy at sea—suppose a ship was approaching. How would you know whether it was a pirate ship or not? Usually by the time you found out it was too late, but if the other vessel fired cannon balls across your bow, you could assume this was a pirate ship and it would be wise to surrender. Could you be sure from the flag? Not at all. Some flew under false colors, flying the flag of another country as a trick.

With those who did fly a pirate flag, anything might do, except for the few who had their own design. Usually, the more gruesome the flag the better to terrorize the victim. Sometimes they were simply of red cloth to signify blood, and that is why we often read the term, "raising the bloody flag." Or the flag might be white paint crudely splashed across a black background. The best-known and most popular flag was the picture of a skull and crossbones, but Blackbeard's flag showed an entire skeleton.

In any case, when a pirate flag was raised the message was death if the captain of the ship did not quickly surrender. The aggressor was usually far better armed. It would go easier on the unlucky captain to accept an invitation to board the pirate captain's vessel, and, of course, it depended on the personality of the pirate as to whether bargaining or some leniency might result. This was not a social invitation. It was an order by the pirate captain to come aboard and give information about cargo and any other ships that might be approaching from the direction whence he had come.

When we begin to research the lives of pirates of Blackbeard's day, we do not have scores of contemporary writers to compare with each other nor the number of sources we would expect to find. It is a surprise to discover that essentially, we have only one contemporary author to consult in researching the Golden Age of Piracy: Daniel Defoe, who produced A *General History* . . . *of the Most Notorious Pirates*. Of course, he chose the boldest and most colorful characters to write about. Writing under the *nom de plume* of Captain Charles Johnson, he produced not only a literary classic but also the basic pirate source work.

Most writers refer to him just as "Johnson," and highly respected as his writing is, even the authority contradicts himself now and then. The contradiction Blackbeard researchers have noted is in regard to Blackbeard's ships—were they lost, or not lost? Johnson stated that the *Adventure* was lost at Beaufort Inlet, and yet this was the same vessel on which Blackbeard was caught in Ocracoke Inlet some five months later. Sources where researchers continue to unearth bits of interesting information are the Manuscript Division of the Library of Congress in Washington, the Research Library of Colonial Williamsburg, Virginia, and the Public Record Office, London.

It was exciting to me to learn that the name of Lt. Maynard's ship in his battle with Blackbeard, which I had searched for everywhere with no success, was discovered recently by Donald G. Shomette, author of *Pirates on the Chesapeake*. Every earlier account gave the name of Maynard's companion ship as the *Ranger*, but it was not until over two and a half centuries later that Shomette, in some of his record searching, discovered that the name of Lt. Maynard's ship was the *Jane*! So much for the difficulties and the rewards of researching this period.

For obvious reasons—such as the risk of being hanged—these buccaneers did not help us by keeping accurate logs recording the names of the numerous ships they sank nor inventory lists of their loot. In fact, the less of this sort of thing found on their ship in the event they were captured, the less there would be to incriminate them. Thus for today's researchers it is sometimes almost impossible to keep up with what ships were captured. Sometimes the pirates would sink a captured ship, in which case it simply disappeared, or they might add it to their pirate command ship flotilla, in which case they sometimes changed the name, sometimes not. For example, when Captain Kidd captured the *Rupparell*, the name was painted out on the vessel and the name *November*—for the month it was captured—painted in. Exit the *Rupparell* forever!

It seems a regrettable lack of imagination, not to mention an inconvenience, that so many ships were named the *Mary Anne*, the *Anne*, the *Pearl*, the *Ranger*, and the *Revenge*. Even for those with the desire to keep legitimate records, it must have been hard to keep them all straight!

Like the ships they plundered or sailed, the pirates themselves sometimes disappeared from the historical record. It should not be surprising that pirates did not form warm and lasting alliances. A notorious pirate like Blackbeard, Bellamy or Vane might be associated during his career with many different pirates who at his request would temporarily command a captured ship. They might later quarrel and part, be lost in a storm, or get killed in an attack on another ship—or the former crew member would simply go out on his own and never be heard from again. To become too intrigued with "what happened" to a temporary sidekick of Blackbeard, Bellamy or Kidd is often only a dead end in the annals of history. (Israel Hands, Blackbeard's sailing master, was one of the few exceptions, for the two had a long-term relationship.) Piracy, like rock music, seemed to spawn a few who were famous and many who dropped into obscurity. A pirate's career could be meteoric, yet end within a few months.

Some of the most successful pirates—whom you will read about in this book—were wealthier than an Al Capone or Dutch Schultz of American gangster fame, and just as cold-blooded. Like their modern-day criminal counterparts, buccaneers were dangerous, unpredictable, greedy men and women. Somehow, these bandits of the sea have been cloaked with more glamor in the eyes of the public than is justified. They deserved to be hanged, and they often were.

Despite the best efforts of New England's Cotton Mather, it was not easy to get a pirate to repent before the hangman's noose descended about his neck. Undoubtedly a few genuinely regretted their deeds. But like some criminals of today, many had no conscience, and the confessions published later would appear to have been composed for them by clergymen in an attempt to discourage others from similar crimes.

For treasure hunters, there are books giving locations where certain pirates are said to have buried treasure. In a sense these caches of treasure were like bank vaults or safety deposit boxes, and like them, their contents sometimes went unclaimed. Of course, the pirates all planned to return, but some were hanged before they could do so, while others died fighting or during a storm at sea. There is no guarantee you will find treasure when you visit a remote island said to have been a hiding place for pirate treasure, but with new and advanced technology your odds are improved.

Remember that only a little while ago in the timeline of history, Blackbeard, John Quelch, Captain Kidd, Charles Gibbs, Stede Bonnet or Samuel Bellamy, from the very spot where you now stand, may have glanced cautiously out over the water as the last shovelfuls of sand filled in the hiding place he had chosen for his riches. And when *you* walk beside the surf, imagine yourself reaching down and picking up a piece-of-eight that once passed through a buccaneer's hands! Don't forget the recent recovery of part of pirate captain Samuel Bellamy's treasure—both coins and jewelry—along with his ship, *Whydah*, only a short distance off Cape Cod at Provincetown, Massachusetts. And off the coast of North Carolina, there is always the exciting possibility that the state's underwater archaeologist's efforts will someday locate one of Blackbeard's ships (along with a hoard of riches!) in Beaufort or Ocracoke Inlet. So keep your eyes open—that glint in the sand really could be gold!

BLACKBEARD
and Other Pirates
of the Atlantic Coast

Edward Teach
New England to Carolina to Florida to West Indies

The early eighteenth century was a time when few of the common people possessed the skills of reading and writing, but Edward Teach, who came from an educated family, was able to do both. He had probably read most of the era's books on exploration and buccaneering, such as *Bucaniers of America* (published in 1679) and William Dampier's *Voyages* (published in 1709).

A native of England's second largest city, the port of Bristol, Teach probably began his own adventures as a privateer sailing out of Jamaica during Queen Anne's War. It was there in 1716 that he joined the crew of the man who would change the course of his life: Captain Benjamin Hornigold. The fiercest, most able pirate of the West Indies, Hornigold was a master tutor in the skills of piracy. "Blackbeard was my star pupil," he would reminisce in later years, referring to Teach by the alias under which the pirate became notorious.

It did not take long for Blackbeard to demonstrate this aptitude. On September 29, 1717, near Cape Charles, Virginia, Blackbeard seized the sloop *Betty* and relieved her of her cargo. Less than a month later, in Delaware Bay, he captured the *Robert* of Philadelphia and the *Good Intent* of Dublin, both taken as they headed up the Delaware bound for Philadelphia. Likely there were others; dates of attacks, and names of ships that Blackbeard seized, went largely unrecorded. Pirates kept no logs.

Before the end of the winter of 1717–1718, Blackbeard fitted out the *Queen Anne's Revenge* and prowled the coast, pillaging ships of all nationalities. During a cruise to the Bay of Honduras, he met Captain Stede Bonnet, whom he invited to join forces with him. The pair sailed back to Carolina, taking numerous prizes on the way. Later Bonnet would learn that there was little difference between being Blackbeard's partner and being the groom of a Black Widow spider. But, for the present, relieved of the responsibility of captaining his own ship, he enjoyed being wined and dined and living the life of a gentleman aboard Blackbeard's sloop.

So prolific were Blackbeard's acts of piracy that whole books have been written detailing his career. Yet his character, his methods of operating, and the fear his reputation inspired all along the coast of the colonies are illustrated in the story of a single incident: his blockade of Charles Towne in 1718.

Near the end of May 1718, Blackbeard braced himself against the rail of his ship and examined the port of Charles Towne through his spyglass. He had spread terror along the entire North American coast, and now his flotilla was strung across the entrance of the southern colonies' busiest port. His powerful body shook with paroxysms of laughter. It amused him that soon frightened people would be scurrying from place to place in the city like ants whose hill had been disturbed.

Teach now called himself "Commodore," assuming authority over all acts on board his armed flotilla of ships. He was king of the sea. His flagship was the 40-gun *Queen Anne's Revenge*, and on board, with a ringside seat, was Captain Stede Bonnet. Lieutenant Richards commanded Bonnet's former ship, the *Revenge*, mounting at least ten guns, and Israel Hands commanded the *Adventure*, mounting eight guns. Accompanying them was a sizable sloop with tenders used by the pirates to transport seized cargo. All together, it was a flotilla formidable enough to terrify any port city.

When the Charles Towne pilot boat came out to investigate, Blackbeard captured it. And then he took a real prize—the *Crowley*, en route to London, with some of Charles Towne's most prominent citizens on its passenger list. Blackbeard was delighted to find among them a member of the Council of the Province of Carolina, the wealthy and important Samuel Wragg, accompanied by his four-year-old son, William. He would have a use for Wragg.

Blackbeard questioned the passengers of the *Crowley* about the number of ships in the harbor, their cargo and destinations, threatening them with death if they did not respond truthfully. Afterward they were returned to their ship and thrust roughly into the cargo hold. All were treated alike regardless of rank, and all were fearful they would not come out alive.

Much of this fear came from the pirate chieftain's appearance. In a day when most men were clean-shaven, the pirate captain wore a monstrous, coal-black beard beginning just under his eyes, covering his entire face and giving him a terrifying appearance. He braided his luxuriant hair in countless pigtails, and before attacking a vessel he tucked lighted fuse cords under the brim of his hat—the same fuse cords used to ignite the powder in cannons. Dipped in saltpeter and lime water, the cords burned slowly, encircling his head with curling wisps of smoke, so that he resembled a fierce demon straight from hell. Crews and passengers of the ships he boarded often surrendered immediately.

Within a few days of his arrival at Charles Towne he and his flotilla seized and plundered eight or nine unwary vessels attempting to enter the harbor, bringing shipping to a halt. No other ships dared come into Charles Towne harbor, and eight who were ready to leave for various ports were afraid to depart.

On the May morning after he had captured the *Crowley*, Blackbeard sat in his cabin with a bottle of rum beside him, drinking and thinking. Some of his men had malaria, some had unhealed battle wounds and some had diseases he was only too familiar with—the price of trifling with women, he thought ruefully. From the chorus of constant complaining the entire crew seemed ailing, and he called in the ship's surgeon.

"And what am I to do?" the surgeon said. "I'm out of tinctures and ointments to treat them."

"Then draw up a list of the medicines we need."

"A list, sir? Where would we get them?"

"I said draw it up!" Blackbeard barked impatiently.

The surgeon obeyed.

"Bring Samuel Wragg up from the hold," Blackbeard ordered. Then he held up his hand to halt the crewmen who had started to leave the cabin.

"Wait! I want these men, too," he growled, surveying the list of passengers' names and placing checks beside some. When all the chosen prisoners had been brought before Teach in his cabin, the pirate spoke in a booming, authoritative voice.

"I am sending two of my men ashore to demand that the Colonial Government of South Carolina supply medicines for my crew. Until they are received, all of you will be kept as hostages. I warn you, if the governor does not meet this demand quickly, I shall order all prisoners put to death and their heads sent to him! The captured ships at the port entrance will be put to the torch!"

The faces of many prisoners turned pale, and some clung to each other for support.

"Who is going to speak up?" Blackbeard said impatiently.

None replied, but they cast glances in the direction of Samuel Wragg, whom they seemed to regard as spokesman. Wragg cleared his throat. "May I suggest," he said, "that you send one of our number ashore with your two men to help convince them of the danger these prisoners are in? That will also prevent any insult to your men from the common people. As to the drugs you require, some may not be available in the province. I hope you will accept substitutions?"

Blackbeard called a meeting of his crew, and in their roughly democratic way, they voted to accept Wragg's amendments.

Now it was a question of who the prisoner should be to go to Charles Towne with the two pirates. Wragg volunteered, and the rest were eager enough for him to go, but Blackbeard immediately vetoed this even though Wragg offered to leave his little son as a hostage. Samuel Wragg was the captain's most valuable pawn in bargaining for the medicine. The Charlestonians might not permit him to return. At last Wragg suggested a gentleman named Marks who was well respected in the city.

"I give you two days to see the governor and bring back the medicine," said Blackbeard. Then he roared, "If harm comes to either of my men, I'll burn every ship in the Charles Towne harbor and ransack the city!"

His frightened face indicating that he believed these threats, Marks settled himself in the small boat between his two pirate companions. Around his shoulders he wore Blackbeard's own scarlet cloak, a sign to the governor that he came with a message from the pirate himself.

Moving the flotilla a few leagues away from land, everyone waited—the prisoners in a state of extreme anxiety. Two days passed, but there was no sign of the trio's return. In a rage, Blackbeard called Wragg before him and accused Marks of treachery.

"I'm not a man to trifle with," he stormed at Wragg. "You and the passengers from your ship prepare for immediate death."

Blackbeard was not easily reasoned with, but Wragg convinced him that South Carolina valued her citizens' lives and that unforeseen events must have caused the delay.

"These prisoners are innocent, and it is not fair to take their lives. The city will redeem them," he assured the pirate. "What is there to gain by haste?"

Blackbeard, still seething, finally agreed to wait another day, warning, "If the boat doesn't return by sundown tomorrow, I will put all the prisoners to death before nightfall!"

The suspense the next day was almost unbearable. The hostages were frantic, and despite the presence of the lookout in the forecastle,

Blackbeard himself spent much of the day pacing the deck, gazing shoreward through his spyglass.

Then came a cry from the lookout. "Small boat coming out of the harbor!"

Focusing his glass on the boat, the pirate chieftain saw something red. It was his scarlet cloak. But when the boat drew up beside the *Queen Anne's Revenge*, Blackbeard and all his men were surprised into silence. The man in the cloak was not Marks. There were no pirates with him, and he had no medicine chest.

Some of Blackbeard's men drew their cutlasses and stepped toward the boat, but their captain raised his hand to halt them. "There will be time enough for that," he said balefully.

The man in the boat was a simple fisherman. Filled with fear, his words tumbling out so hastily they could scarcely understand him, he tried to explain.

"On the way to Charles Towne the gentlemen's boat was caught in a sudden squall, sir. She capsized, and your two men with Mr. Marks swam to an uninhabited island. The pirates—I'm sorry, your two gentlemen—placed Mr. Marks on a hatch and, swimming behind it, tried to push him toward the city. If I hadn't seen an object floating in the water and sailed toward it, all three men would have perished."

"And what did he and my two men do when you pulled them out?" asked Blackbeard with suspicion.

"Mr. Marks hired a boat to Charles Towne. He paid me to sail out to you and explain."

Blackbeard scowled, but even in his frustration the story seemed to ring true.

"Let this fellow have food and rum to put some backbone in him," he said with a sardonic look at the still frightened fisherman, "and give the prisoners the run of the ships. I won't execute them for probably two days. What do you think, Israel?"

"I'd give 'em twenty-four hours, if 'twas up to me."

"It isn't."

Entering his cabin, he spent the rest of the evening drinking with Israel Hands. Another officer joined them for a mug of Jamaican rum—a powerfully built, princely figure of a man everyone called "Black Caesar."

When the two days of grace passed with no sign of an approaching ship, Blackbeard's rage was terrifying to all on board. Striding back and forth beside the rail, he swore that the governor of South Carolina had thrown his two men in jail. He vowed to kill all hostages and flay alive any South Carolinian he could get his hands on. Gradually Wragg calmed him and convinced him to let the prisoners live until next morning. "The envoys may return during the night," he reasoned.

By now some of the prisoners were completely unnerved. "Do the people of our city think a chest of medicine is worth more than the lives of eighty of us?" they muttered amongst themselves. In their desperation, many of the men from the *Crowley* made the pirates a shameful promise, saying, "We will pilot the ships into the harbor and join you in attacking the town!"

The capsized boat had delayed Marks and the pirates, not all the listed medications were available and substitutions had to be decided upon. There was no intentional effort to delay. But Blackbeard was not noted for his patience. He called a meeting of the pirates, who agreed that the time for waiting was past. The four fighting ships along with the four captive ships sailed into Charles Towne harbor and ranged themselves into a line facing the town. On shore the people were now suffering the same terror that the prisoners on the *Crowley* had endured for several days. All knew they were about to be attacked by the coast's most frightening pirate.

Meanwhile, the governor's council was meeting. The governor didn't want to sacrifice the citizens on the *Crowley*, and he fully realized how defenseless the city would be if Blackbeard attacked. The harbor was completely unprotected, and there was no warship within hundreds of miles. The council agreed to meet Blackbeard's demands, and the medicines they could supply were assembled.

Ready to embark with the chest, Mr. Marks searched everywhere but was unable to find the two pirates—a further delay. He could not return to the ship without them, and he knew Blackbeard would think that they had been jailed or harmed. A general alarm was sent out, and they were soon found with some drinking companions visiting one pub after another—happily, uproariously drunk.

On Marks's return, Blackbeard released the captured ships, their crew and passengers—half-naked. Much to these prominent gentlemen's embarrassment, they had been relieved of their handsome clothes and personal finery, which the pirates now sported with delight.

Blackbeard's fierce threats and reputation as the most bloodthirsty pirate of the Atlantic coast had reduced a proud city to submission without the firing of a single shot!

The medicines were of no great value; the pirates could have asked for real treasure and probably received it. But they had plundered eight or nine ships during the blockade, and in addition to being heavily loaded with cargo, the hulls of their ships held kegs and chests of gold and silver. Blackbeard was returning to Ocracoke, North Carolina, with one of the most valuable hauls of his career. The blockade had not been unprofitable. Gold and coins from Wragg himself amounted, some say, to 1500 pounds sterling, not to mention seven or eight other ships plundered during the blockade.

As other pirates accepted the king's offer of pardon, surprisingly enough Teach decided that he would too. Less than a month after his highly profitable blockade of Charles Towne, he and his crew appeared before North Carolina governor Charles Eden and surrendered. He took the same oath his old mentor Hornigold had taken earlier—the promise to be from then on a law-abiding citizen—and began the life of a wealthy gentleman.

A pretty planter's daughter had reformed this fierce pirate, thought the wedding guests in Bath as they stared at the tall, burly captain beside his lovely 16-year-old bride. Teach's finery outshone that of the girl and was in marked contrast to the sedate clothes of the distinguished gentleman conducting the Anglican marriage ceremony—Governor Eden. The governor might have dropped his prayer book had he known that Mary Ormond was the groom's fourteenth bride!

Blackbeard strolled the streets of Bath Town, courteously answered naive questions about pirating and appeared to enjoy his new role. But this content was short-lived. Within he chafed at the dull social life, the tame card games played by the planters and the conversation of men who considered the most momentous journey of their lives a trip to Edenton, North Carolina. Soon Blackbeard began to ask himself what he was doing in Bath Town. Was he to spend the rest of his life here in the doldrums?

He thought about Hornigold. How was that infamous old brigand of the sea faring? Did he yearn for the excitement of seeing a prize on the horizon, of testing his mettle in battle against that of other men, and of the heady sensation of power on seizing a vessel?

Teach himself was as restless as a caged lion, and so were his crew members who remained in Carolina. Only the presence of the captain himself in their midst kept these idle, rowdy ruffians from bringing chaos to the province. It was easier for the captain to handle them on shipboard. After the vice-admiralty court in Bath Town gave Teach a clear title to the *Adventure* to use in trading on the high seas, he took his old crew back to sea, having applied for and received clearance to set sail for St. Thomas. There were sighs of relief from law-abiding people that the pirates would be gone for awhile, but at the same time they were a bit regretful, for they knew that Blackbeard's presence protected them against other pirates. When the *Adventure* sailed Captain Teach carried two documents on board: his certificate of registration, and his proof of a "gracious pardon" for piracy.

Back to sea he went, attacking any ship that crossed his path, sometimes putting in at plantations along the Carolina coastal rivers to hide or provision his ship. Sometimes he paid for his provisions—to give the impression that he was an honest seaman on a trading voyage—but his charade of respectability went no further. Blackbeard had no intention of going to St. Thomas; instead he headed north to Philadelphia to see old cronies.

He had quaffed rum in the taverns on the Philadelphia docks for only a few days when he learned that Governor William Keith of Pennsylvania knew of his presence and had issued a warrant for his arrest. He was as well known on the waterfront of Philadelphia as in the coastal towns of Carolina.

Blackbeard immediately left for Bermuda and on the way met several English vessels. Since he had not had time to re-provision his ship before his hurried departure, he robbed the English ships of only what he really needed and let them go. Two French ships that he met next were another matter. One was empty, the other laden with sugar and cocoa. Putting the crew of the loaded ship aboard the empty vessel, he left them to go on their way and sailed off with the vessel full of sugar and cocoa, making for his favorite anchorage at Ocracoke Inlet. A month later he reported to Governor Eden that he had "found the French ship at sea without a soul aboard her," he and several crew members signing affidavits to verify the claim.

The governor convened a vice-admiralty court, and the court's decision declared the ship a derelict found at sea—with Tobias Knight, chief justice and secretary of the colony, presiding. Knight was awarded 20 hogsheads of sugar and the governor 60 under the laws of salvage for a derelict ship on the high seas. For all the court knew at that time, the ship really had been a derelict, and the verdict did not prove any dishonesty on the part of either Governor Eden or Knight.

Meanwhile, in Virginia, Governor Spotswood needed to play the hero. He was facing opposition from the majority of his own council—possibly a crisis in government. To capture Blackbeard would improve his image enormously—not to mention his financial resources, for he was convinced Blackbeard possessed an enormous treasure. He was lucky enough to arrest William Howard, Blackbeard's quartermaster, in a Virginia town and to extract from him the location of Teach's North Carolina hideout and the fact that at present he had only a few men. Declaring to the people that the pirates had threatened to avenge themselves on Virginia for convicting Blackbeard's quartermaster and sentencing him to be executed, Spotswood worked the colony into the state of alarm required for his plan.

Keeping his intention secret even from his own council, who would not have approved his methods—and who were by now openly opposing him on other matters—the Virginia governor planned to invade North Carolina. Spotswood leased two sloops at his own expense and promised a generous bonus from the Virginia Assembly over and above any other reward seamen who volunteered would receive for capturing Blackbeard. The governor did not give the Virginia Assembly time to approve legal action. Spotswood's two armed sloops slipped secretly out of Hampton on the afternoon of November 17, 1718, under the command of a Lieutenant Maynard. Between the two of them the sloops carried about 53 men and a trained fighting crew from the Royal Navy.

Lieutenant Maynard arrived at Ocracoke Inlet as the sun was setting on Thursday, November 21. The mast of Blackbeard's ship could be seen just over the dunes in the last glow of the afternoon light. The *Adventure* was anchored where it always was, on the sound side of the southern tip of Ocracoke Island. Since Maynard had no pilot who knew how to navigate the shoals, he decided to settle down and wait until dawn of the next day to attack.

That night, unaware of impending battle, Blackbeard drank with the master of a trading vessel and three of his men who were on board visiting. For six months there had been little activity and no attention from any seagoing vessels, who probably considered the pirate retired. His ship had only a skeleton crew of about 18 men, most performing menial tasks—probably few of them even skilled at using a cutlass. It is doubtful he considered it important to post a sentry.

Before sunrise Lieutenant Maynard ordered the anchors raised and headed toward the tip of the island and the waters of the sound. As dawn broke, a rowboat left Maynard's ship, the *Jane*, to precede the sloops, take soundings and signal the course. When the *Adventure* saw the rowboat, Blackbeard's crew fired a round of shot, which sent the boat scurrying back toward the sloops. The two sloops made a formidable enemy, and Blackbeard certainly guessed that they had more men and the odds were against him. He could have evaded the two English sloops, escaping through the inlets and channels he knew so well, but that was not his nature. He was not a coward. The *Adventure* headed straight for the two sloops. Hoisting the Union Jack, they tacked directly toward the pirates, and the fight was on.

Blackbeard, the master navigator, amazed his own men by slowly changing the course of his sloop and heading for the Ocracoke beach! The *Jane* and the *Ranger* followed, unaware that Blackbeard was entering a narrow channel beside a shallow, hidden sand bar, and both grounded themselves. Now they were close to the pirate vessel, and Captain Teach himself roared across the water.

"Damn you for villains, who are you? And from whence come you?"

"You can see from our colors we are no pirates," Maynard shouted back.

"Send your boat on board so that I may see who you are," ordered Blackbeard.

"I cannot spare my boat, but I will come aboard you as soon as I can with my sloop," came back Maynard boldly.

Realizing they were going to board by force, Blackbeard seized a bowl of liquor, quaffed from it generously, then shouted at the officers of the sloops: "Damnation seize my soul if I give you mercy or take any from you!"

"I expect no mercy from you. Nor shall I give any," Maynard retorted.

This was brazen talk, since both Maynard's ships now lay on the sand bar and the crews were struggling to dislodge them. Blackbeard signaled for his men to fire, and the *Adventure*'s eight cannons leveled a broadside at the grounded vessels. Four blasted the *Ranger*, putting her out of action, and about 20 men on Maynard's ship were either killed or wounded by the other four guns. Blackbeard had now reduced the force attacking him by half. But the tremendous thrust from the *Adventure's* guns sent the pirates aground, too. Blackbeard began trying to refloat his ship. Meanwhile, Maynard, knowing a volley from the pirate's guns might destroy his vessel at any moment, hurried desperately to get her back into action. He threw the water barrels and the ballast overboard. Suddenly a breeze sprang up, and all the ships were able to push away from the sand bar.

With some men wounded and others killed by the pirate's volley, the battle with Blackbeard might well be a disaster, but Maynard would not turn and flee any more than his opponent. Instead, he decided to try an old ruse of sea warfare. Leaving the fallen bodies of those killed by the cannon shot on deck, he ordered all his surviving men below, with weapons ready. They were to remain in the hold. If the pirate was to fight, he must come and get them.

Blackbeard saw Maynard's ship approaching and alerted his men to get out the grappling irons, ready their weapons and be prepared to board. At the same time he had a surprise for the Royal Navy: hand grenades his men had made by filling bottles with gunpowder, shot, and pieces of lead, to be set off by fuses worked in the center. When the grenades struck the deck of the *Jane*, there were loud explosions and dense clouds of smoke. When the smoke cleared, Blackbeard saw only a few living men and a number of bodies on the sloop's deck.

"They were all knocked on the head but three or four," he cried joyously. "Blast you—board her and cut them to pieces!"

The *Adventure* nudged the side of the Royal Navy sloop, and as it did the pirates threw the grappling irons across the bulwarks. Teach leaped aboard among the bodies of the dead seamen, not knowing these were only the ones killed by his cannon fire. He had just tied the rope to make fast his own ship and the other vessel when he heard shouting and shooting, and to his surprise saw Maynard's men begin pouring up from the hold.

A fierce hand-to-hand combat began as men slipped and slid in the blood on the deck. There were shouts and shrieks, the clatter of swords striking each other and the sharp sound of pistols firing. Into the fray waded Blackbeard, wielding his great cutlass in an arc that struck the blades of the English aside. Maynard fought his way toward him until the two men met.

Each pulled a pistol and fired. Blackbeard's shot missed. Maynard's struck and went through the pirate captain's body but did not fell him. The captains began to battle with swords, and Blackbeard struck Maynard's weapon with such force that the blade snapped off. Now vulnerable, all Maynard could do was hurl the hilt at Blackbeard while the pirate closed in, swinging his cutlass to make the kill. But as he did, a British seaman struck the pirate from the rear and, says Johnson, "gave him a terrific wound in the neck and throat." The pirate chieftain's raised cutlass swerved, striking only Maynard's hand. Blackbeard staggered and almost fell, recovered himself and, despite the blood gushing from his neck, continued to fight with the ferocity of a wounded bull. British seamen afraid to get too close to his gigantic swinging cutlass saw that he was weakening from all of his wounds, and began to stab him from the rear with their swords.

As he was cocking another pistol, the mighty pirate captain finally died, but not before proving himself a man superior to others in talent, cleverness, courage and strength. Maynard later found that Blackbeard's body had suffered five pistol shots and no fewer than 20 severe cuts. Writing of his death, Johnson said, "Here was the end of that courageous brute who might have passed in the world for a hero had he been employed in a good cause." Maynard ordered Blackbeard's head severed from his body and suspended from the bowsprit of his sloop, then had the pirate's body thrown overboard.

Legend has it that when the headless body of this man of such strength and determination hit the icy water, it swam around the sloop three times before it sank.

It is said that over the years Blackbeard buried his enormous treasure in many places. One of these was Smutty Nose Island among the Isles of Shoals. Natives of the area tell a story that he once returned from England with a beautiful girl, and while he buried the treasure, she explored the island. Surprised by a man-of-war, he hurriedly sailed away and left her. In vain she waited for his return until her death. Natives of Portsmouth, New Hampshire, say her ghost haunted the island for nearly a century.

Ocracoke Island off the North Carolina coast has long been considered Blackbeard's headquarters. The Outer Banks provided countless inlets ideal for pirate concealment, and "Teach's Hole" was a place pirates often congregated, one to be avoided by honest seamen. The buccaneer also frequented a group of islands farther south near McIntosh, Georgia, and one of them was named "Blackbeard's Island" after him.

Stede Bonnet
*Pennsylvania to Virginia
to Carolina to West Indies*

I n the late morning he rode his black stallion at a deliberate pace along the winding, dirt road of the plantation, fringed on either side with lush green banana plants. The tropical sky was an intense blue and the sun so bright it hurt Stede Bonnet's eyes—not surprising, because Stede Bonnet had a hangover. But it was not his fault. He was driven to drink by the boredom of this blasted place where one day was much like another. What excitement could there possibly be if a man never had to overcome danger or risk his life?

Barbados had all the appearance of a paradise, but to a man with a reckless, adventurous spirit, this island of cane and banana plantations, a civilization that had gone virtually unchanged for more than a century, was a provincial prison.

And if he should complain to his wife or his sisters, what would he say he wanted instead? What would they see as a reasonable alternative? Their reaction to his desire to leave the island would be one of horror and despair, but not so great as if he told them his *secret* desire.

Yet what was there to lose, he thought, for a man already dead within?

He turned his horse's head toward the Bridgetown dock as he was often wont to do. Captains of the ships taking on sugar, rum, molasses and more dubious cargo glanced at him curiously as he sat astride his black stallion watching them. A man in fitted black trousers and a loose white shirt with full sleeves, he was dressed a shade too flamboyantly. He had dark, curly hair, a suntanned skin and regular if not handsome features. The seagoing men who put in at Barbados knew *his* kind—a wealthy, pampered sugar plantation owner amusing himself; a scion of one of the English families who enjoyed a life of ease in the pleasant climate of this small South Atlantic island.

Barbados had only recently become a British colony. The war with Spain was over, and Governor Lowther represented the crown. The governor spent his time trying to encourage trade at Bridgetown harbor while discouraging the lawlessness that remained from the decade before; it had been here that dashing privateer captains, dressed in silk and velvet and ornamented with gold chains, had anchored to dispose of captured cargo.

Stede Bonnet, mounted on the black Arabian stallion, thought of those days on this sunny spring morning of 1717. Although to his fellow islanders Major Bonnet appeared to be a typical planter—the steady and responsible husband of Mary Allamby Bonnet and father of their children, Allamby, Edward, Stede and Mary—in truth he was the very opposite. The staid example his father had set him in his youth had long ceased to do battle with a self of another sort, one who took wealth and ease as his right and now sought only excitement.

At 12 he had visualized himself as a swashbuckling knight-errant living by the sword. Many boys have such dreams but reject them with maturity; however, Stede was now 28 and his admiration for men who seized what they wanted from life by force had not waned. It had become an obsession. In the afternoons he read, stared moodily at the masts of the ships in the distant harbor or went down to the docks and sat astride his horse watching vessels come and go, daydreaming about adventure.

To anyone in such a state of mind, fate inevitably presents an opportunity to choose the course of his secret desire. So it was that

Stede Bonnet learned of a vessel up for auction.

"Found deserted at sea without papers or crew," said the captain who brought her into port—an unlikely story! She had probably been taken in an act of piracy the year before. Major Stede Bonnet was high bidder. The major's wife and his friends in the port village were puzzled, but he explained that he had decided shipping would be a logical extension of his sugar and rum production.

Friends queried him hopefully. "Will you be buying rum or sugar from us? You will need more than you can supply from your own plantation, if you're to prosper in this venture."

He would smile mysteriously and make no reply. Major Stede Bonnet was planning to embark on a career of piracy. He knew what that meant. When a state of war does not exist, armed robbery at sea is regarded as a crime against all men. He would be an international outlaw—a criminal who could be tried and hanged anywhere in the world.

Although Bonnet knew nothing of seafaring, he hired a quarter-master who did, one Israel Morton, and Morton began to recruit men. Meanwhile, even Bonnet's wife did not realize that the sloop her husband had dubbed the *Revenge* was now ready to accommodate 70 fighting men as a pirate ship.

The sun had not yet risen one morning in late June of 1717 when a carriage pulled up at the dock, and the black driver leaped down to take off two small trunks. He held out an arm to assist his passenger. The man who dismounted might have been attired for a fancy-dress ball. He wore a rakish black felt hat, a full-sleeved shirt, a brace of pistols, and a cape. His black boots gleamed in the lantern light. The servant lifted two trunks into a small quay. There was a gentle splash as the boat pushed off, and soon all that was visible was a dark shape in the stern as the small craft slid quietly through the water.

Aboard the *Revenge* it was soon apparent to the crew that their captain, with his ruffled shirt front and lace at the wrists, was something of a dandy and no seafaring man at all. Luckily for the major, the experienced Israel Morton had looked out for his interests.

The quartermaster had screened all members of the crew before hiring them to be sure that they were the sort of men who would turn pirate given the opportunity. Now he watched as Bonnet stood before the crew assembled on deck.

The major was unaware that he presented an almost comic figure as he raised his ruffled fist and shouted, "From now on this is a pirate ship, men, and I expect you to take every damned vessel we can find."

"Every red-blooded man who will join us in getting rich, step forward," put in the quartermaster fiercely. Morton had confided to key men in the crew that he was prepared to break a few heads if any of the men showed opposition, but that proved unnecessary. The entire crew stepped forward. He had chosen well.

On their part, the men were filled with excitement. As was the habit of pirates, they set about electing their own officers. They voted in Morton formally as quartermaster, and with his urging, the swashbuckling Bonnet as captain. Later that day they voted on the pirates' Articles of Agreement.

Now Stede Bonnet paced the deck in great elation. In a few days he would show the crew what sort of captain he was! And he did. He began to order the quartermaster to tie men to the mast and lash them for breaking minor rules. A more serious infraction elicited the terrible penalty of marooning. With deceptive gentleness he would go up to the offending seamen and say, "I shall make you governor of the next deserted island we see!" Struggling and protesting, the seaman would be forcibly put off the ship at that island and left to die.

For awhile the luck of this "gentleman" turned pirate was phenomenal, and his reputation for cruelty became so widespread that the reward for his capture exceeded even that of Blackbeard. It is said that despite the tales told of pirate horrors, Stede Bonnet was the only buccaneer who actually made his prisoners walk the plank.

Off the Virginia Capes Bonnet came upon the *Anne* from Glasgow, Scotland, and the *Turbet* from Barbados and seized them both. The latter vessel was unfortunate to have come from Bonnet's home port, for he ordered her burned to the waterline to keep word of his activities from reaching home. Although the seamen of a captured ship were usually offered the opportunity to join the pirates, there is no record of the fate of the crew of the *Turbet*.

The next vessels to be captured by Bonnet were two English ships, the *Endeavor* out of Bristol and the *Young* of Leith. Then he headed for South Carolina and Charles Towne, where the sea trade was heavy and the riches to be obtained by looting were enormous. On the way he captured a brigantine from New England and a sloop from Barbados.

Now his ship needed cleaning, for her sides and bottom were heavy with barnacles. Morton found a suitable location, and the crew went to work right away. Careening a ship was a dangerous task that had to be done quickly—ideally in less than 48 hours—for a ship on its side was highly vulnerable. The cleaning safely completed, the pirates took a vote on where they should sail next.

Then the men of the *Revenge* made a bold move. They voted to head for the Spanish Main—the northern coast of Colombia and Venezuela—and gold. It was a fateful decision.

Bonnet had been back at sea for only a day or two when he met another pirate ship. It was customary for pirate captains who were friends to fire cannon salvos to greet each other when they met. In this case, however, the pirates had never met, and civilities were exchanged instead. Bonnet stood staring across at the other ship, uncommonly impressed at the sight of the huge, broad-shouldered, ferocious fellow leaning against the rail eying him through binoculars.

Although most men of the day were clean-shaven, this man's face, up to the eyes, was submerged in a black beard of the most extravagant length. He was dressed in black with a broad-brimmed hat, knee boots and a veritable arsenal of pistols hung from a sling over his shoulder. The broad belt around the man's waist held more pistols and daggers along with an immense cutlass.

Stede Bonnet recognized this man with considerable shock. He was facing the most awesome member of the Brethren of the Coast,

Captain Edward Teach—or Blackbeard, as many called him.

Blackbeard invited Captain Bonnet over to his ship, plied him with drink and then suggested that they join forces. He made the point that two pirate ships, working together to stalk and overtake their prey, were more efficient than one. Bonnet, believing that Blackbeard must be impressed by his reputation, accepted the invitation, and the two vessels continued on their way in quest of gold. Between Guadaloupe and the Virgin Islands, they seized several ships loaded with valuable cargo.

But as they maneuvered, closed in, attacked and boarded the ships together, Blackbeard became contemptuous of Bonnet, quickly seeing him as a man who had no skills in handling either a ship or a crew. Captain Teach knew of several methods to dispose of this liability.

After inviting Bonnet on board for a dinner where liquor flowed copiously, Blackbeard warmly patted his friend on the shoulder and told him that the luxurious quarters on *his* ship would be far more suitable for a man of Bonnet's standing and gentlemanly background. Blackbeard suggested that if a rougher sort of fellow from his own ship, such as Lieutenant Turner, took over the captaincy of Bonnet's ship, it would result in a more lucrative arrangement for all. A liquor-befuddled Bonnet agreed, and the next day Bonnet's crew voted for Turner to replace him as their captain.

There were still two pirate ships, but now there was only *one* crew and over it, one commander: Blackbeard. Communication with other vessels was swift, and the news of what had happened was shouted across the water from ship to passing ship until Bonnet's humiliation was the joke of the coast.

The career of the man who would a-pirating go had received a severe setback. He still came and went as he pleased but made no decisions, seldom joining the men in their pleasures ashore. He spent his days reading and brooding. It was obvious to him as to everyone that Blackbeard had no intention of assigning him any responsibility.

For a time, Stede Bonnet saw his folly and was full of shame when he thought of what he had done as a pirate. If this insight had been lasting and if true repentance had occurred, Bonnet's future might have been very different; however, his chagrin was only a symptom of his natural inclination to sulk when frustrated.

Now Blackbeard, loaded with loot, cast about for ways of eliminating men who would normally share it. Turner rejoined Blackbeard, who instructed Bonnet to return to his ship and go into Bath Town to surrender to Governor Eden and receive the king's pardon.

"I will rejoin you soon and do the same. Then we will divvy up the loot," Blackbeard promised him.

Major Bonnet went to Bath Town and was absolved of all his deeds by the governor, but Blackbeard never appeared. In fact, he did not even approach Bath at all but sailed away, and a furious Bonnet never laid eyes on the loot or his "friend" again.

Shortly afterward, the pardoned Stede Bonnet was seen no more in Bath Town and a "Captain Edwards" appeared on the deck of the *Revenge*, sailing north upon the high seas. Bonnet thought his new name would conceal his identity and someday even enable him to go back to Barbados as Stede Bonnet. Later, he changed his name again, dubbing himself Captain Thomas—perhaps for his grandfather and uncle, who were both named Thomas.

In July 1718 Bonnet anchored the *Revenge* off Cape Henlopen, Delaware, and shortly after nine that evening he and his crew were delighted to see a large ship drop anchor in 14 fathoms of water at the mouth of the river. "Captain Thomas" sent five men hurrying off in a rowboat to seize the stranger.

The mate on the deck of the *Francis*, who would be well able to testify later, described what happened:

> I saw men approaching in what seemed to be a canoe, and I thought they were probably friendly. I called out to them saying, "Where are you from?" One of them hollered back, "Captain Thomas Richards from St. Thomas and Captain Read from Philadelphia." Then he asked, "Where are you from?" I answered, "Antigua. You are

welcome to come aboard," and I had a man lower a rope
to them.

As soon as the strangers came aboard they clapped their hands to
their cutlasses and roughly shouted, "You are taken!"

The pirates then forced the *Francis*, along with the *Fortune* which
they had seized the day before, to sail with them out of Delaware Bay
and south toward the Carolinas.

"Captain Thomas" was in high spirits. Although still angry about
Blackbeard's trick, he was regaining his confidence and reveling in
his success at his newly resumed career.

"Gold is gold no matter how you've got it," he had always said,
"whether by privateering or piracy." He looked years younger now
than when he had left Blackbeard and sailed into Bath Town. He was
a man for whom excitement was the breath of life and danger an
intoxicating stimulant racing through his veins. He relished the
discovery of each new vessel and the attack. He also prided himself
on being a much more experienced seaman than on that early
morning when he left Barbados in his first ship.

Today he took the wheel himself and with his two prizes, the
Francis and the *Fortune*, sailing on either side, he pictured himself
lining his pockets with gold. It did not occur to him, as he sailed out
of Delaware Bay, his men carousing and guzzling rum punch, that he
was about to make the worst decision of his career.

Since the *Revenge* was entirely too well known as a pirate vessel,
"Captain Thomas" now renamed her the *Royal James*. She had not
been cleaned in some time, and Bonnet must find a place to careen
her. As luck would have it, she was also leaking and repairs would add
to the time the vessel was helpless.

Arriving at the mouth of the Cape Fear River, the pirates decided
to sail upriver to an isolated cove and careen the sloop. If Bonnet had
been as experienced as he thought he was, he simply would have
changed to one of the two captured vessels with "clean heels." Both
were in better condition than the *Royal James*.

As Bonnet's crew worked, citizens a little farther south were girding themselves against new pirate attacks. Of the southern ports that had been victimized by pirates, Charles Towne had suffered more than most. The vicious Captain Charles Vane had terrorized Charlestonians, and not long afterward Blackbeard had audaciously laid siege to the city. Now there was word that Captain Vane had returned! In fact, he had sacked a small vessel from Antigua right in sight of Charles Towne harbor.

Before releasing the crews on these ships, Vane had slyly hinted that he was planning to sail south, put in at one of the rivers and stay on in the area. This was a ruse to delay any vessels who might set out after him, for Vane was actually going to leave immediately and sail northward. The misinformation had been carried to Colonel William Rhett, who was ready to give hot pursuit.

Meanwhile the *Royal James* was still attending to maintenance. Cleaning and repairs had taken much longer than Bonnet had estimated. Life as a buccaneer had its drawbacks. One was being unable to seek parts and repairs in a harbor that offered these services to law-abiding vessels. Quartermaster Morton had gone to scout for what he needed in Charles Towne. It was not easy to find replacement parts, and the pirates had to capture a small ship in the river and salvage what they needed. The prisoners they released went to Charles Towne and reported that pirates were careening in the Cape Fear.

Everyone hearing this news was convinced the pirates were Captain Vane and his crew. But before Colonel Rhett went up the Cape Fear he took advantage of a wind from the north and sailed southward, thinking Vane might already be on his way. Of course, there was no sign of him, since the wily captain had headed north. Colonel Rhett now slowly sailed up the Cape Fear in search of the careened pirate ship.

Suddenly, he saw his pirates ahead—not one, but three ships lying at anchor near a spit of land. In their eagerness to reach them the pilots of both Rhett's ships ran aground in shallow water. There was no way to get back afloat until high tide. It was too late that night to approach the ships more closely.

By now the pirates had seen the masts of Rhett's ships, and their first impulse was to set out by night to capture them. But what they saw, after paddling through the water in the darkness, was not the unarmed vessels they expected but rather 16 mounted guns on two large sloops. They scurried back to report to Bonnet.

That night Stede Bonnet prepared for battle, transferring all arms and prisoners to his ship and abandoning the other two. At daylight when he made a run for it, Rhett's two sloops headed toward him, hoping to board. Colonel Rhett was flushed with excitement, believing that Charles Vane, who had all of Charles Towne aroused, was within his grasp. He could see himself returning with the notorious pirate captain as his prisoner.

Bonnet sailed sidelong toward shore and grounded his ship. Now it was impossible for Colonel Rhett to keep the *Royal James* between his ships, and the result was that both the *Henry* and the *Sea Nymph* also ran aground—but not in quite the position Rhett would have chosen. They were parallel to the *Royal James*, and both were in gunshot range.

As the tide began to fall, the pirate ship listed to port, providing cover for the pirates to shoot from behind the starboard rail, while Rhett's vessel listed toward the *Royal James*, exposing the men on Colonel Rhett's deck to devastating gunfire from the outlaws.

The firing continued six hours. Neither side was able to use cannon, for Bonnet's cannon was aimed toward the sky and Rhett's was aimed toward the water. At last the *Henry* floated free and began to move toward the pirate vessel. Bonnet shouted over the speaking trumpet, "Stay where you are. I'm sending a flag of truce aboard you." Rhett was enraged that they thought he would surrender.

The truce party boarded, and Colonel Rhett could hardly conceal his surprise when he found that the pirate captain did not ask for his capitulation but wanted to surrender to *him*. Dazed, Rhett accepted as Bonnet surrendered himself, his ship and his crew.

Rhett had an even greater shock in store for him. He now realized that his captive was not Charles Vane! The prisoners from the two ships the pirate had captured immediately identified him as the infamous Captain Stede Bonnet. Rhett took him prisoner and delivered him to Charles Towne.

In that gracious port city, Bonnet's treatment was most courteous, and he and two of his men were even placed under arrest at the marshal's home rather than the prison. Yet the fact that he would have to stand trial, even though the death penalty was not expected, so enraged Bonnet that he and one of the crewmen, dressed in women's clothes, escaped and set out northward in a small open boat. They had little food or water. The weather suddenly became stormy, and the pair was forced to turn back to Sullivan's Island. Here Rhett captured Bonnet again, and this time the attitude of the authorities toward the pirate captain was harsh. He had forfeited the sympathy some Charlestonians had previously held for him as a "gentleman."

His own men testified to the ships he had taken and his crimes. They were later hanged, and a jury found Bonnet "guilty as charged."

Even a desperate letter in which Bonnet pleaded his new conversion to Christianity did not move Governor Johnson, who well remembered that Stede Bonnet had the blood on his hands of numerous other murders in addition to those that had convicted him. Nor did Johnson forget that on an earlier foray into the Charles Towne harbor Bonnet had threatened death and destruction to the city. The escape attempt only confirmed that the pirate couldn't be trusted.

In his letter to the governor, Bonnet nevertheless begged to be made even a menial servant to his Honor and asked that his life be spared for "the reputation of my family." Ironically, he had not communicated with that family since he had left Barbados.

Wednesday, December 10, was set as the day of execution. From the time Major Bonnet, dressed in his lace-trimmed clothes, had stepped into the boat at the Barbados dock until the tenth of December of 1718 his life of excitement, danger, bloodshed and violence had lasted only a little over a year. As one once favored with wealth, the company of the best society on Barbados and the respect of his friends, he now seemed a rebel without a cause.

As the time for his execution approached, Bonnet was in such a state of terror that he could neither sleep nor eat. The prospect of death unnerved him. The appointed day dawned clear and sunny. Outside the watch house where he was imprisoned, Stede Bonnet could hear a steadily increasing roar of voices. A crowd was gathering. The hanging of a pirate was a public holiday, and entire families came from the countryside around to make a day of it. He heard the voices of hawkers selling food and drink. But the dreaded sound was yet to come. He knew what it would be like, for he had heard it each time one of his men was taken away. He waited with apprehension. Then the creaking wheels were there. It was the hanging cart, come for him.

A crescendo of shouts rose from the crowd: "Get him. Bring him out!" He heard the scrape of the jailer's boots on the stone floor approaching his cell. He couldn't make his legs work, and two smelly, burly men grabbed him roughly, carrying him along, his feet barely touching the ground. They hoisted him into the vehicle. He thought it would take him straight to the gallows, but instead the horse drawing the cart turned in the opposite direction.

The route was to be a circuitous one, turning down several Charles Towne streets so the assembled crowd could see him pass. Boys followed the cart, thrusting their jeering faces up at his. Some spat upon him. In all his dreams of glory he had never anticipated this! Suddenly a little girl ran up to the cart and thrust a bouquet of wildflowers in his hands. Her mother jerked her back.

When the horse and cart finally drew up at the gallows, the crowd became quiet, eagerly awaiting his last words. Mouth dry, he opened his lips to speak, but no words came. The crowd waited. Would it be something impudent, some unrepentant statement, or a word of warning to the men in the crowd on the folly of becoming a pirate? These people would be hard to surprise. They had heard it all from other pirates.

Bonnet's entire body was trembling as if with ague. He opened his mouth a second time, but no words came. Now the people let out a roar of contempt and disappointment. To hear a man's last words before he died was one of the most thrilling parts of a hanging, but all Captain Stede Bonnet could do was sit in the cart, shaking, unable to speak a word! Urchins shouted insults and hurled pieces of discarded food at him, hoping to get some response. None came.

The cart moved forward toward the gallows, and Bonnet looked up numbly at the dark noose silhouetted against the blue South Carolina sky. For the first time he spoke. "Oh my God, oh my God," he repeated over and over.

The hangman placed the noose around his neck. He heard the crack of a whip on the horse's rump. The cart jolted out from under him, and with a searing collar of pain around his throat Stede Bonnet felt himself hanging in mid-air.

As he writhed in the torment that followed, there were seconds when the past streamed through Bonnet's brain—rides down lush green avenues of tropical plants . . . shaded plantation house rooms . . . the burning heat of the sun in the blue sky . . . family faces . . . everything gone now in a nightmare of agony and slow death at the end of the hangman's rope miles from home. Brightly colored fireworks burst behind his eyes, sparks soaring, flying, falling, fading, into eternal night.

Even after his death convulsions ceased, the captain's manacled hands clutched a tiny bouquet of flowers. Then the fingers relaxed. Israel Morton stepped quickly forward, picked the bouquet up and melted back into the crowd.

The "Gentleman Pirate" was no more. His body would be left hanging there for four days.

Thomas Tew
New England to Red Sea

R ichard Tew arrived from Northampton, England, to settle in
Newport, Rhode Island, in 1640. There he founded a respected
family, and there he left descendants for 350 years. Of them all, one
would be notorious.

Arriving in Bermuda some 50 years after his grandfather had
settled in America, grandson Thomas Tew made no secret of his
distinguished background, and whether he had family money or had
obtained his wealth through certain enterprises of his own, he spent
gold freely. He let it be known that he did not wish to follow in the
footsteps of his respected grandfather. The esteem of other men
would have to be gained in his own way.

Some saw a reckless streak in him, but at the same time he possessed
such engaging warmth and forthrightness that men trusted him
despite rumors about his past. He was popular on the island and, along
with a group of prominent men, including a member of the Governor's
Council, Thomas Tew purchased a share in a fine sloop. Privateering
was a thriving business in 1691, and Tew lost no time in convincing
his fellow part-owners of the *Amity* that a privateering commission
should be obtained from the governor. The commission was granted,
and Captain Tew, as he was now called, easily found a crew.

When he sailed from Bermuda another privateer, commanded by

a Captain George Drew, accompanied him. They were instructed to take a French factory at Goree beside the river Gambia on the west coast of Africa, but on the way a violent storm came up, Captain Drew's sloop sprung her mast, and the two vessels became separated. After the gale subsided Captain Tew held a meeting of his crew and told them that the attack upon the French factory would be of little value to the public and would not reward them with booty. "Privateers" were strictly admonished to capture only vessels from a country with whom their country was at war. Seizing the ship of any other nation was piracy.

"I only took this commission in order to have employment," he went on, "and I think we should consider how we may better ourselves. If you want me to I can take a course that will lead to a life of ease for the rest of our days."

His crew was well aware this was an invitation to become pirates.

"A gold chain or a wooden leg—we'll stand by you!" came a unanimous answering shout. The men cast their vote for piracy. Instead of Gambia they now set their course for the Red Sea, and then had only just entered the Strait of Babelmandeb when they saw a large, heavily laden Arabian vessel approaching. It appeared well manned, but Tew told his crew that it would contain a fortune and that even with all the mounted guns and soldiers, the Arabian crew would prove poor fighters.

True to Tew's word, they took the vessel without losing a man, and the amount of gold and jewels was fantastic. Each man received a share amounting to about 3,000 pounds sterling. Other vessels also became fair prey.

Arriving at Madagascar, so great was their wealth that the quartermaster and 23 others elected to leave the ship and settle in a remote island area to enjoy the pleasant climate. The rest of the crew stayed with Captain Tew, thinking that they would now head for America. However, the contours of the land had scarcely disappeared behind them when they saw a sizeable ship. Tew visualized all of them returning even richer, and, firing to windward of her, he hoisted the black colors. Unexpectedly the stranger fired back at him to leeward.

Sending out a boat, Tew learned that he had intercepted the famous pirate Captain Mission, who had a privateering commission from France. Aboard the *Victoire*, Tew was sumptuously entertained and then invited to visit the pirate colony, Libertatia, that Mission had established.

So it was that Tew and his men were soon following Mission's ship into the harbor at Libertatia. They were surprised to notice how well fortified the place was. At the first fort they were given the courtesy of a nine-gun salute, and when they arrived on shore the company there greeted Tew and his men hospitably.

The two captains got along famously, and Tew was invited to a conference to decide what to do about a large number of prisoners Mission had brought back with him. Seventy-three of them—both English and Portuguese—joined the pirates, and the others were sent to work on a dock that was being constructed just above the mouth of the harbor. Meanwhile, New Englander Tew and his men settled in nicely. It was a well-established society. Libertatia had its own flag, the people called themselves the *Liberi* and they had built houses, forts and public buildings. Farms were large, many raised cattle, and they added to both their population and wealth through piracy.

Tew was profoundly impressed by Mission's goals for Libertatia—a society with no class distinctions, where all would be equal. Mission was already carrying out these ideals and promises. All captured slaves were freed at once and given land or an occupation. Schools were established, and the ignorant were taught French and English. Booty taken from expeditions was equally divided among those who remained ashore and those who went to sea.

Here was a man Thomas Tew could admire—the very opposite of his father and grandfather, in whose eyes a man's political office or wealth determined his position in the world. Mission, a charismatic French nobleman, had exchanged a life of luxury and ease for his dream of building a utopian society.

Tew's hero had not begun as a captain, but when the previous captain of the *Victoire* had been killed in an engagement with a British ship off Martinique, Mission had assumed command, making his friend Caraccioli, a former priest, his lieutenant. The pair had fought a fierce and successful battle to take the English ship, and as a result the crew had unanimously acclaimed Mission their captain.

Ex-priest Caraccioli was an accomplished fighter. In addition he was an atheist and a socialist. His persuasive eloquence had converted Mission and most of the ship's crew to his beliefs in equality, liberty and humanity.

"Men were never born to be slaves," said Mission to Tew, echoing his mentor. "The rest of the world may brand us as pirates, but it will be through their own ignorance."

It was a bizarre company, a multi-racial crew led by an idealistic Frenchman, a renegade priest and now a New England pirate, Captain Tew—all of them filled with ideas which they were ready to force on others through powder and gunshot.

Tew's crew stayed on among the colony, enjoying their new friends. But an argument arose between Tew's men and Mission's original French settlers, and the two leaders decided the only way it could be settled was to fight a duel. At the last moment the diplomatic Caraccioli intervened, pointing out that the loss of either man would be irreparable. The underlying friendship and respect each man had for the other made them see the tragic consequences of settling differences in such a way.

"To avoid further quarreling our state must elect rulers and frame a constitution and laws," said Caraccioli.

Mission was unanimously elected Lord Conservator with the title of Supreme Excellence, Thomas Tew was made Admiral of Libertatia and Caraccioli was appointed Secretary of State. Pirates and settlers then elected a house of representatives without discrimination regarding color or wealth. All cattle and treasure was divided equally, and those with no knowledge of farming were given work they could do at wages regulated by the state. There was no chance for graft.

At this point Captain Mission, deciding it was time to strengthen the colony, offered Tew command of an expedition to go to Guinea and seize whatever the pirates required. This trip to Guinea was a success, and Mission sent Tew on many others. Through such expeditions, settlers in Libertatia were joined by Dutch, French, English, and Portuguese, and ships were sent to faraway ports to secure these new recruits.

On one of these voyages Admiral Tew was north of the Cape of Good Hope when he sighted a Dutch East Indiaman with 18 guns. He boldly seized it, losing only one man and gaining several chests filled with English crowns. Nine Dutchmen joined him, and the rest were set ashore in Soldinia Bay. Off the coast of Angola, Tew took an English slaver with 240 blacks aboard. His black crew members were overjoyed to find some of their relatives among them and told of their happy life in Madagascar where slavery did not exist.

"Remove their leg irons," ordered Tew, and his ship returned home with the blacks, where they set to work on the dock.

Determined to map the waters around the island, Tew spent his next voyage sailing around Madagascar in a sloop called the *Liberty*, charting shoals and taking soundings of water depths off the treacherous coast. It was four months in the doing.

Then an even more imaginative and ambitious project occurred to the admiral. He would establish a trade route between his home in Rhode Island and their pirate kingdom. He was already a prosperous man, but this route could greatly benefit Libertatia and attract the world's attention to the unique society Mission had established. Tew first set sail for Bermuda, but a gale springing his mast set him off course. After two frustrating weeks of bad weather he decided to sail directly to Newport. Arriving there a week later, he was received with great respect, especially when it was discovered how wealthy he had become.

In Bermuda, the co-owners of the *Amity*, who had heard nothing from Tew for two years, were waiting apprehensively. Would they receive their share of the vessel's booty? Tew immediately dispatched a request to the other part-owners to send an agent for their money, and a sloop arrived at Newport in a few weeks. It was commanded by a Captain Stone, who testified some years afterward that he took back French dollars and Arabian gold amounting to ten times the worth of the vessel. The Bermuda owners were generously repaid.

Meanwhile Tew was successful in obtaining a new privateering commission to "seize the ships of France and those belonging to the enemies of England." Leaving Rhode Island, he sailed south, rounded Cape Horn uneventfully and was soon at anchor back in Libertatia. There he found that the colony needed men more than riches, so he set out on a cruise to the Red Sea. His ship, the newly fitted-out *Victoire*, carried a crew of about 250 men.

The first place he stopped was a settlement started by his former quartermaster and certain of the men who had left Libertatia. Coming to anchor, he went ashore to urge them to rejoin the colony. The quartermaster—who now enjoyed the title of "governor"—was friendly, but he and his men had everything they needed and were enjoying their freedom from a world of responsibilities.

The "governor" and Tew were drinking punch together that afternoon when suddenly a storm came up with so high a sea that Tew could not get out to his ship. The storm grew more violent by the minute, and Tew saw that *Victoire* was moving toward a steep point of the island. She had parted her cables. The gale drove her ashore on the point, and Captain Tew watched through his glasses in anguish while his crew was swept overboard and drowned. He could give them no assistance. There was nothing to do but stay and hope that Captain Mission would eventually come in search of him.

A few weeks later two sloops anchored offshore and from one of them a canoe came ashore. It was Captain Mission. Tew was greatly relieved, but he dreaded having to tell of the loss of the *Victoire* and her entire crew. To his surprise, before he could speak, Mission embraced him with tears in his eyes.

"In the dead of night we were attacked by an island tribe," the Frenchman said. "They came down upon us from two directions and with their machetes they slaughtered men, women and children." Tears slid down Mission's face unchecked. "We never harmed them," he went on, "yet they showed our people no mercy."

The absence of the 250 men with Tew and the sailing of another ship in the harbor had so weakened the little colony that the men in Libertatia had been overwhelmed just by the tribesmen's numbers.

"Caraccioli died fighting," Mission said sadly. "I managed to escape but with only forty-five men." He had brought with him a considerable weight of rough diamonds and bar gold.

Tew pointed out where his own ship had gone down, and the two men consoled each other. Neither of them had ever wanted to wipe out all the natives of the island, even had that been possible, yet they realized now how vulnerable their small model society had been. It was the end of the dream. They grieved, each in his own way, for Libertatia and for Caraccioli, the firebrand of hope who had inspired them.

"Let's abandon this roving," urged Tew. "Come with me to America where all of us can live in comfort and safety."

But Mission would not dream of going anywhere until he had first returned to France for a visit with his family. Dividing between himself and Tew the diamonds and gold, he then gave Tew one of the sloops, and they sailed. Mission had 15 Frenchmen and Portuguese in his sloop, and 34 Englishmen accompanied Tew. But still tragedy stalked them.

Before they reached the Cape the winds rose. Tew adjusted his sails and saw Captain Mission do the same. Sails shrieked like baleful banshees as wind tore at them. Tew saw Mission's sloop list heavily to one side in the storm. Would the sea broadside her? He waited for her to right herself. Within seconds she keeled over on her side, and he saw Captain Mission's vessel disappear into the black maw of the tossing sea. She had been only the distance of a musket shot away, but the distraught Captain Tew could give no assistance. It was all he could do to shout orders to his men and keep his own sloop afloat. Above the storm and wrenching noises of his own vessel, Thomas

Tew shouted his rage and grief and shook his fist at the sky.

In Newport, Tew's house with its captain's walk was lavish indeed, and the captain enjoyed its beauty. After his crew received their share of diamonds and gold, they had quietly dispersed. He lived a tranquil life, now and then seeing one of his men, Thomas Jones, who had married Penelope Gulden, a young lady of a good family. He only wished the others had adjusted as well.

The way of life was too quiet for many of his old crew members, for they had squandered their money, and they had no interest in a trade or fishing or farming. After a year or so they began showing up at Tew's door in Newport more and more frequently to recall the "old days." They tried everything in their power to persuade him to go back to sea.

At last they came in a body to the house. "Just one more voyage, captain," they begged.

At first Tew refused, but finally he weakened.

He was so confident of securing another privateering commission that while waiting for word of it he was busy in Rhode Island fitting out a sloop. On his periodic trips to New York to dispose of diamonds, he and Governor Fletcher had become friends, and it was to that "gentleman" that Tew had applied. His request was granted—and the governor was to share the booty. Fletcher's honesty was highly questionable, and his dealings with pirates were well known. The privateering commission would be a cover for Captain Tew in many encounters with other ships.

A few months later Tew sailed from Newport in a sloop he had sentimentally named the *Amity* for the first ship in which he had sailed from Bermuda. He was joined by a Captain Want in a brigantine and a Captain Wake, an old pirate who had been pardoned. Want was Tew's mate on the first voyage in November of 1694. Tew went around the Cape of Good Hope to Madagascar to take on food and water and from there to Surat, Mecca and Tuda to lie in wait for traders.

During the next few years, whenever he returned to the Atlantic coast, Tew would go to one of the places—Carolina, New York, New England or Rhode Island—where pirates had always been well received.

Captain Tew soon acquired a fleet of several ships, and an Englishman's letter to London reported that one of his ships had left Boston, another New York, and another Pennsylvania, while two each had departed North Carolina and Rhode Island. When Tew's ships returned to the Atlantic coast they would conceal their sloops in the uninhabited harbors of Carolina and the islands off the coast of New Jersey or Pennsylvania where they felt safe. And treasure? They brought chests of it so heavy it took six men to hoist them, and no one was there to question whether these riches had come from a friendly or enemy nation.

Tew was so successful that he never had any trouble attracting a crew. Now and then he thought of retiring to his house in Newport but visited it rarely. Perhaps he became a prisoner of his crew's constant thirst for wealth and excitement.

In the late 1690s he headed once more for the Red Sea. As usual, he sighted prey quickly—a Moorish ship he surmised was rich with treasure. He ordered his men to fire, but for the first time the Moors offered unexpected resistance.

Suddenly and horribly, a shot from the Moorish guns tore away part of Tew's stomach. In the words of a contemporary writer, Daniel Defoe, he stood stoically on deck and "held his Bowels with his Hands." He stood thus for some time. Then finally dropping them he collapsed and died, his death striking "such a Terror in his men, that they suffered themselves to be taken, without making Resistance."

And so Captain Thomas Tew departed this world far from his native state. In less than a decade, he had lost his dream of an island utopia, his good name and his opportunity to live out the rest of his life happily in his Rhode Island home.

Descendants of the Tew family may still be found in the Newport area today, but they do not wish to talk of the captain.

John Davis
St. Augustine, Florida

John Davis, alias Robert Searles, was one of those men who inspired the Spanish to declare that all Englishmen were pirates. A respectable privateersman, with a letter of marque permitting him to attack enemy ships, a pirate he became.

Clever, with the ability to act swiftly and seize his opportunities, Davis engaged in piracy for a number of years. By April of 1688, however, he had become restless. There was a certain monotony about capturing one ship after another—plundering a vessel, then mopping up the bloodied deck if he decided to keep it or, if that was impractical, sinking it and disposing of the crew in a reasonably humane way.

Often, some of the captured crew would join him. Others tried but had no stomach for it; and then there were those so honest that they indignantly resisted his invitation to become buccaneers. He had seen all these reactions so many times.

On this April day, Davis found himself looking out over the sea as the sun rose, sighting a sail on the horizon and thinking, *Well, another day, another frigate. Is that really all there is?* He longed for a new kind of adventure.

Seizing a ship one morning on the way bound from St. Augustine, Florida, for Havana, he found a surgeon on board and discovered that the fellow was at least good company. He didn't fall into any of the usual categories. They took their evening meals together, and Davis began to see that the French doctor had an obsession. He had served the garrison at Ft. Augustine and was consumed with hatred for the Spanish governor, Guerra. As captain and surgeon drank together at night, Dr. Pedro Piques talked about Guerra at length.

"I told him plainly that his womanizing was a scandal and reminded him that the church had warned him about it from the pulpit."

"And what did he say to that?" Davis asked, mildly interested.

"He said, 'You're fired!'"

"Fired? As garrison surgeon?"

"Yes. Then he drew back his hand and slapped me on the side of the face." The Frenchman brought his fist down on the table, shouting, "No man can do that to Pedro Piques!"

"And so?"

"I asked for my pay—almost 200 pesos—and he approved it. But afterward the rascal railed at me, 'You're no Spaniard, you're a Frenchman. I don't need to pay you anything.'" Dr. Piques, who had lived in Spain most of his life and spoke Spanish like a native, gave a furious snort at the remembered insult. "But I shall get my revenge."

"And how do you propose to do it?" asked Captain Davis.

Piques, undecided, had no answer. His unruly grey eyebrows drew into a furious frown, and his face grew red with anger as he continued bitterly.

"You can't imagine the luxury in which this man, Guerra, lives." He leaned forward and spoke emphatically. "There's great wealth in St. Augustine."

Now Davis' pale blue eyes glinted like the sea with the sun upon it, and he listened more intently. His eyes rested on Monsieur Piques' shirt—the beauty of its fabric, the rows of ruffles down the front, the lace at the cuffs. The surgeon saw the direction of his gaze.

"You should see the fine clothes those Spaniards wear," he remarked.

"Like the shirt you have on?" asked Captain Davis with obvious envy.

"Of course. Silk shirts and velvet breeches—finery like the apparel ladies and gentlemen wear at court in Madrid. Oh, there's gold in St. Augustine."

"Then the fort must guard the city well?"

"No, and that is the ridiculous thing. The Spanish take few precautions."

"Have they ever been attacked?"

In a flash Piques saw his opportunity for revenge. But he replied casually, "No one would dare. They boast continually of their fighting prowess."

At this Davis smiled and lay back indolently in his captain's chair, his strong, beringed fingers straying to the hilt of his cutlass as if he were already rising to a challenge. "They do, do they?"

Piques nodded. "Yes. They're an arrogant lot. Incidentally, what kind of fighter are you, Davis? Didn't you take a ship or so after you left Jamaica?" Now the doctor was baiting the captain. He already knew that Davis, fresh from a series of triumphs off the coast of Nicaragua, was feeling his oats.

"Well, I do have something of a reputation as a fighter," said Davis with pride. "This Castillo de San Marcos—you say it's not very strong?"

"Strong! It's built only of wood and is actually tottering."

Musing, Davis stared out to sea. "A strategic place, St. Augustine."

"Certainly it is—right at the exit of the Bahama channel."

"All the trading ships between the Indies and Spain use that channel," said the captain, twirling his mustache thoughtfully.

"No wonder the town is wealthy," said Dr. Piques. "It could be a lucrative base."

Davis had withdrawn his cutlass and was testing its sharpness with his finger, and then he spoke.

"I'll need your help, my friend."

"Help?" The surgeon felt his heart leap.

"In planning my attack on St. Augustine."

Piques tried to conceal his elation. "Will your men agree?"

"Of course."

Despite Davis' confidence, however, the crew's vote was without enthusiasm. A ship they would gladly attack—but an entire town, with a fort and unfamiliar places for the enemy to hide? That was different.

Once he had the crew's vote—however unenthusiastic— Davis began to consider his strategy, but found it difficult to develop. For the life of him he was unable to plan further than entering the harbor and landing his men on the least populated side of the town. Unlike an attack at sea, where the response of his victims was much more contained and predictable, a land attack had many possibilities, and Davis was uncertain what he would face.

Piques, discussing the plan with unconcealed delight, gloated over his approaching revenge.

"Seizing the *Nueva España* was very fortunate," he reminded the captain. "You can use her to approach the town, and the watchtower will see she's a Spanish vessel. They're expecting a shipment of flour."

"And we will be that shipment of flour." Davis grinned. He loved deception.

"As we enter the harbor the watchtower will ask for your identity," warned Piques. "How will you answer?"

"In Spanish, of course," Davis replied with a smile.

The morning of May 28 Davis ordered his helmsman to steer toward the harbor and anchor two leagues from the inlet. Ashore an alarm sounded and the pirates could see the harbor pilot coming out in his launch.

"Identify yourself!" the pilot shouted to the ship.

"El situado! We bear the money to pay the troops."

Davis had forced a Spanish prisoner from the *Nueva España* to reply—persuaded by a knife against his ribs. Suspecting nothing, the pilot boarded, and Davis immediately took him prisoner. That afternoon the captain sent one of his own men out in the pilot's launch to take soundings in the inlet. This caused no misgivings at St. Augustine. Soundings were a common procedure before a vessel was guided in. Someone might have wondered why the ship remained at anchor long after the tide and southeasterly wind were ideal for her to enter the harbor, but no one seemed to notice.

Piques seethed with excitement. Vengeance was only a few hours away, and his hatred for the governor overshadowed any concern he might have once had for former friends on shore.

Captain Davis did not hurry. The attack he planned would take place that night, and he could already taste victory. Piques had given him one of his ruffled shirts with lace at the cuffs, and he had wound a golden yellow silk sash about his waist. He wanted to be impressively dressed, for he would soon be in charge of this strategic fort and its settlement. By nine that night it was dark enough to dispatch another frigate from his flotilla, and Davis manned it with pirates. He hoped the approach of the frigate would not cause the watchtower to become suspicious.

In the tower at Matanzas Inlet the men saw a small vessel approaching St. Augustine and sounded an alarm. Soldiers arrived on the alert. Reminding themselves that they were expecting *two* ships—the flour shipment, and a local frigate returning from Havana—the men in charge of the watch decided these were the Spanish vessels.

Governor Guerra suspected nothing. He ordered the soldiers to leave their weapons at the main guardhouse with the ordinary guard. "Go home and go to sleep," he ordered, and they did.

In the cabin of his ship, Captain Davis imagined how his capture of such a strategic place for his headquarters would be talked of and envied by other pirate chieftains. It was time for the first step of his plan. He ordered his men to pull the pilot's launch and that of the *Nueva España* along with two pirogues beside his vessel.

"Where's the pilot of the harbor launch?" he asked, and two of

Davis's crew thrust the protesting man forward.

"Lead us to St. Augustine," Davis charged him, "and I warn you, if we run aground you won't live to remember it."

Davis sat down behind the pilot in the launch. Piques and about 100 of the captain's best men embarked with him. Following the advice of the surgeon, Captain Davis had his men row along the west shore of Anastasia Island and up the Sebastian River. They would anchor on the uninhabited side of town and, at daybreak, attack. Their objectives would be the governor's house and Fort Castillo de San Marcos.

"It will be a quick victory," Piques confidently assured the captain. Davis did not reply. He had more than enough courage, but his element was robbery on the high seas—not on land. On a ship he knew every place someone could spring out at him, every compartment where a man might lurk to escape his cutlass.

Not long after midnight, as they glided across the waters of Matanzas Bay past the more settled part of St. Augustine, Davis sensed the presence of someone nearby. In a moment he heard the sound of oars.

"Turn the launch toward shore and hurry," he whispered to the pilot. Davis soon saw the outlines of a fisherman's canoe with a figure paddling desperately. The launch started skimming swiftly after it. Now the canoe reached the surf and was nearing shore. The captain raised his revolver and aimed. A first, then a second shot rang out. A man's scream shattered the quiet as a figure leaped from the canoe and ran toward the fort.

Davis and his crew streamed ashore, most of them running toward the main guardhouse. Other pirates raced down the streets of the town as men and women emerged, confused and sleepy, from the doors of their homes. By the light of torches the people saw the wild figures of the pirates running toward them—rough-voiced men with broad, flopping hats, many-hued coats and bright sashes or belts stuck full of long-barreled pistols and heavy knives. They swarmed noisily along the St. Augustine streets, opening fire with their pistols, killing and wounding anyone in their path, and forcing their way into the houses. Estefania de Cigarroa, the daughter of the mayor, ran out of her home with her little sister in her arms. A bullet killed the younger child and pierced the older girl's breast.

Piques seized Davis' arm, propelling him at a run in the direction of Government House.

"Guerra—we'll find him over there," shouted the surgeon above the din. He was eager to finish off the governor with a quick thrust of his dagger to the jugular. Messy, thought he; but his hatred, like a rush of molten lava, could no longer be contained, and he longed for the sight of Guerra's blood.

The captain, meanwhile, was becoming breathless. Used to the deck of a ship when he attacked the enemy, his feet were seeing more action than his sword arm. What was he doing sprinting down the dirt road of this village?

As they crossed the plaza, Piques gave an exultant shout.

"There he is! See him—on the stairway at the side of the Government House."

The surgeon fired his revolver, but the bullet struck far wide of its mark. Captain Davis opened fire and missed the governor by inches. Guerra dashed back in just as his secretary came out of the building, and Davis's bullet struck the secretary instead. With pirates at his very heels, Guerra escaped through a false door and reached the fort. Sending out messengers, he ordered his soldiers to report to the Castillo immediately.

"Forget the governor!" Captain Davis barked impatiently at Piques. Leveling a stream of oaths at his men, who had begun to plunder the town, he ordered, "Get over to the Castillo and open fire!" But still they tarried over their loot. "Open fire on the fort!" he bellowed with rage and fired a few shots over their heads.

Inside the fort, the Spaniards were struggling to load the cannon, but before they could do so Davis and his men attacked. For an hour and a half Captain Davis tried to scramble up the outside walls of the fort. He longed for the rope ladders of a ship's rigging. His feet slipped time after time, and he and his men were forced back by the heavy musket fire raining down upon them. Finally Davis heard the explosion inside of a powder barrel going off, and he ordered a withdrawal.

He counted 11 of his men dead and 19 wounded and ordered his remaining pirates to regroup and watch the fort, but whenever his head was turned they slipped away to continue looting the town. From a distance he watched helplessly as almost 80 Spanish soldiers arrived to reinforce those inside. His foray on land would soon prove a disaster. Shouting and cursing, he again exhorted the pirates to gather and attack the fort.

But some were already streaming toward the boats carrying sail canvas, wax candles, silver marks and priceless ornaments from the village church. Others were still coming out of the houses bearing valuable utensils and jewelry. Pirate ships had been brought in and anchored in the harbor, and boats began going out to them laden with booty.

It was soon obvious that Davis' men had no desire to stay behind and occupy the town. They were not colonists. They were not settlers seeking permanent responsibilities or power. They were robbers and rovers with a desire to fight, seize their loot and leave. The captain's dream of capturing and holding a town was disintegrating before his eyes. By now Davis was disgusted by the very thought of governing these silly townspeople who were running about in such a panic. He began to realize that this would be the worst sort of bondage for a man like himself who made decisions on the spur of the moment and came and went as he pleased.

Returning to his vessel in the bay, he found the deck a scene of chaos, for the pirates had brought aboard about 70 men, women and children, including the town treasurer and the parish priest. What was he going to do with all these people? The fort's cannon was now firing at the ship.

He wished he could go, but some of his own men were still somewhere on land. He was also faced with a shortage of food. He had never had this many problems when seizing ships.

By nine o'clock his crew had straggled back to the ship. After a meeting with those who were sober enough to discuss what should be done, Davis decided to promise the safe return of prisoners and give his word that the women's honor would be kept intact, if the town would provide him with an ample supply of water, meat and wood.

The governor accepted, and the captain, as a sign of good faith, released the women first. He put the other captives ashore when the food had been brought out to his ship. After six long days the pirates could at last set sail toward the mouth of the bay. Then, from the ship's wake, came the sound of a voice shouting. "Help, help!"

They looked back to see a man swimming desperately after the ship.

"Isn't that the doctor? Your friend?" a pirate shouted to Captain Davis.

Davis held his glass up to his eyes, scowled, and then turned his back on St. Augustine and the swimmer. His binoculars swept the sea to the east. Was that a sail? Yes! He gave a deep sigh of satisfaction. He could feel the familiar surge of excitement mounting within him and a certain joy. Yes, joy! The challenge he knew so well lay ahead.

"Trim the sails!" he shouted exultantly, and the pirates sped out to sea.

Nor does history record that Captain John Davis ever invaded a town along the Atlantic coast again.

Charles Vane
New York to Carolina to Florida

When Captain Charles Vane saw the large merchant ship, he immediately began to consider how he could take it—the vessel was better gunned than most. His approach, as always, was a friendly one. He and the master, Captain Holford, began talking back and forth, and after the two had sailed the same course for a day and a night, Holford invited Vane and several of his officers over to celebrate. Holford's own crew was drinking heavily, and before long someone let slip that they were carrying a rich cargo.

Later that night, Robert Deal, the first mate, knocked on the door of Vane's cabin.

"Do you know what Holford is carrying?" Deal asked.

"I have no idea," said Vane. "What is he carrying?"

"Some say gold!"

"Well, we must be more hospitable—invite him over tomorrow night and break out our best rum and brandy."

They decided that when Holford's crew was sufficiently drunk, Vane would give the signal, and his men would overpower the captain and kill him.

The sun was well up by the time Vane and most of his crew had slept off the effects of brandy, rum and cognac. A short time later a small boat set out, and the invitation was duly delivered to Holford.

"Tell your good Captain Vane I shall be delighted to come," replied the crafty Holford, who at one period in his life had been a buccaneer himself. After the seaman turned to go, Holford winked at his first mate.

"He has heard that we are carrying gold," the captain said. "We must be alert for a trap."

By early afternoon a fog began to drift in, and under its cover Holford slipped anchor and was gone. When the fog finally lifted, Captain Vane realized what had happened, but Holford was too far ahead to pursue even had Vane known his course. It would be some years before their paths crossed again.

A tall man with a rakish hat pulled over his eyes stood at the rail of his sloop, watching as two men-of-war cruised into Providence harbor. From his own ship, Captain Charles Vane saw the tall man. "It's our fine new governor," he sneered, a smirk crackling across his face, tanned as a dried persimmon.

"He means to clean out all the pirates, I hear," said the quartermaster.

"Let the milksops and cowards crawl to Governor Rodgers for their certificates of pardon," Vane snorted. "We'll not do so!"

After sunset Vane and his crew slipped their cable and glided toward a prize vessel anchored near them in the harbor.

"Raise the colors, men!" he shouted. The skull and crossbones slid up the rigging and began to flutter in the May breeze. Vane fired insolently—a nose-thumbing gesture—as he passed one of the British men-of-war on his way to sea. Since most of its crew were filling themselves with ale ashore he knew he was safe from reprisal. Sailing southward for less than 48 hours, he captured a sloop from Barbados which offered no resistance, and placing a drinking buddy, Seaman Yeates from Carolina, in command, he sent him aboard with 25 crewmen.

A few days later a small but trim little Spanish trading vessel appeared in their path. Vane's men lined the rail of their sloop, daggers glinting in the sunlight. Hoisting the pirate flag, Vane intercepted her. Once again the frightened crew, who had been bound for Providence, offered no resistance, and Vane's men boarded the vessel.

"Stay on shipboard, Yeates. I'll search her myself," Vane called arrogantly across the water. Yeates paced up and down the deck of his vessel, swinging his cutlass and fuming at being humiliated before his men.

Vane was delighted to find that the Spaniards were carrying a quantity of silver which they had fished up from the wrecks of the galleons in the Gulf of Florida. Some of the silver found its way into Vane's own pockets before he took the bags back to his ship and divided them. He tossed a small chamois bag over to Yeates, who knew he was getting table scraps. Since he did not need more men for his own crew, Vane took the Spanish vessel and put the excited, protesting Spaniards ashore on the next island to fend for themselves.

On he sailed until he saw a small island well suited to cleaning his ships. For almost a week they worked on the ships by day and caroused by night; but the need for fresh provisions was acute, and in the latter part of May the pirates headed for the Windward Islands.

Because there had been no time to provision the ship before leaving Providence, Vane's men had been living off of the supplies of the ships they had seized. Since these schooners had almost reached port when attacked, they had been carrying only small amounts of fresh food. Now Yeates' crew was coming down with scurvy, the ration of liquor was dwindling, and the men on both ships were surly.

Yeates still resented Vane's arrogant way of relegating him to second place, as well as the unequal division of the gold—against the rules adopted by the pirates themselves. He voiced his discontent, and the feeling spread among his crew.

Vane sensed danger. If grumbling developed into plotting there was always the possibility of mutiny. Now, cursing the time wasted on the island, he blamed all his problems on Yeates. While he was fuming and trying to decide what to do, he spotted, through his binoculars, a small sloop on the horizon. A better view of it convinced him it was another Spanish vessel—probably bound from Puerto Rico to Havana. As they drew within hailing distance the Spaniards shouted greetings, but seeing the number of men on Vane's and Yeates' ships, they soon became quiet. Large crews usually meant a pirate vessel, for they were much more heavily manned in order to attack other ships. Cargo ships carried only a few men.

Drawing alongside, Vane's men quickly threw their hooks over the rail of the Spanish sloop and boarded, only to discover that some of the Spaniards had scurvy, and much of their cargo was inedible. They opened one barrel after another, cursing as the contents spilled, and they discovered that they were little better off than before. Fights broke out between the pirates and the captured crew, and several Spaniards were injured.

Captain Vane, to show the captives the mettle of the man they were dealing with, pointed out the first mate.

"All right, men, keelhaul him!" Yeates protested the need for this, but Vane ignored him. "Keelhaul him!" he bawled angrily.

Vane's crew passed ropes under the hull, tying one to the culprit's feet and another to his arms. "Now, throw him overboard!" shouted the captain.

The Spaniard was pulled underwater from one side of the ship to the other, cut each time by the razor-sharp barnacles clinging to the hull. Finally, Vane tired of this ugly sport and had the man pulled up on the deck. Yeates had seen men keelhauled before, but he saw no sense in inflicting punishment on a man who had not offered armed resistance. Hardened as he was, at the sight of the brutally cut and bleeding man, Yeates felt sick.

In an ugly humor, Vane ordered the pirates to put the semi-conscious man and the rest of the crew into a small boat.

"Now. Set their ship afire!" Flames and sparks soared high into the air, and, jeering at the helpless men in the dory, the pirates sailed away, leaving them to die.

Late that afternoon an unsuspecting brigantine and sloop appeared on the horizon, and the spirits of the pirates rose. Seizing both vessels, they found fresh vegetables, fruit, pickled fish, dried meat, flour, brandy—just the cargo they needed for a sea voyage. Now they could continue their travels, and so they did, sailing and taking vessels as they went.

Finally the ships reached Carolina. Here the pirates took several vessels, one a large brigantine from Guinea with about 90 blacks aboard. Despite lack of space, food and hands to take care of them, Vane insisted on loading all the blacks aboard Yeates' vessel. Yeates was furious.

Making no further pretense of cooperating with the captain, Yeates and his crew met together, deciding that at the first opportunity they would either seek a pardon for piracy from the governor or strike out on their own piratical ventures without Vane. Then there would be fewer with whom to divide the loot. Many pirate captains were trustworthy about apportioning the shares of the booty, but Captain Vane was clearly not one of them.

Suspicious of Yeates, Vane took two of that ship's crew aboard his own sloop, where they were threatened and tortured. At last they confirmed that Yeates planned to leave him at the first opportunity.

Yeates slipped his cable that night and sailed, and the angry Vane began to chase him. His brigantine was the speedier, and he had almost overtaken him, when Yeates, seeing his former captain within gunshot, fired a broadside at him, heavily damaging the brigantine.

Safely arriving at the mouth of the North Edisto River south of Charles Towne, Captain Yeates, disillusioned with his career of piracy, sought the governor's pardon for himself and his comrades. "We will surrender ourselves to your mercy," he wrote, "along with our two sloops and a cargo of blacks."

The return of the blacks may have influenced the South Carolina governor the most, for they were valuable property and had been taken off a ship belonging to a Captain Thompson. Yeates's request for mercy was immediately granted, and he sailed into the port of Charles Towne.

Outside the harbor, an angry Captain Vane lay in wait, ready to catch Yeates and murder him when he emerged. But the pardoned Yeates, who never reappeared, was glad to end his minor career in piracy and his brief association with Charles Vane.

Captain Vane had to satisfy himself with seizing two ships bound for England—then Vane released these ships after stripping them of provisions and equipment. One of the ships, returning to port to re-equip, met Colonel William Rhett, whom the governor of South Carolina had sent out with two well-armed sloops to capture other pirates in the area. The schooner captain reported that his ship had just been plundered by Captain Vane. He said he had heard from the men who had been prisoners on board that the pirate was heading south.

Rhett, who had been sailing north, quickly changed his course—and thus fell victim to the deception that Vane had planned for just such a situation. Vane had purposely allowed the prisoners to hear that he would be going south to throw off any pursuers. He actually stood away to the north.

Had Rhett pursued his original course, he might have captured two pirates at once, for in an inlet further north, Vane met briefly with the infamous Blackbeard. Vane saluted his fellow buccaneer, his great guns loaded with shot. This was the custom among pirates when meeting, even at some distance from one another. Blackbeard responded, and the two men exchanged news, then went on their separate ways, Captain Vane continuing north.

October was a month of beautiful weather, and Vane and his crew were not pressed for food. While he was off Long Island, Vane was tempted by a small brigantine and a sloop, both easy game, but after that it was a month before the pirates sighted any other vessel. Then they encountered a ship which elicited cheers. It was a fine prize!

"Hoist the colors," urged Vane, and the black flag went up. He looked for a quick surrender but was surprised when he was struck by a broadside from the other ship's guns. As the French colors went up on that ship, Vane saw she was a man-of-war, a heavier vessel with many more guns than his, so he trimmed his sails and stood away. But the French ship, setting all her sails, had a mind to pursue and came after him.

Crew member Jack Rackham, a reckless sort who would later prove infamous in his own pirate career, believed they could board the man-of-war, show themselves the better fighters and take the ship. Mate Robert Deal and about 15 of the crew stood with the captain. Vane argued that they might be sunk before ever being able to board the boat, and even if they did board, the vessel they would be attacking had twice as many men. Since the captain had final say in matters of fighting, chasing or being chased, Captain Vane prevailed. A crisis was averted—for the time being. Later, Rackham and Vane again disagreed, this time over the division of a ship's spoils and the manner in which Vane lorded his captaincy over Rackham. The two separated, Rackham taking some of Vane's crew with him.

Vane next set a course for the bay of Honduras. Cruising off Jamaica, he took a sloop and two piraguas. All the men from the captured vessels joined them, and Robert Deal was appointed captain of the captured sloop.

In February Vane and Deal set sail from the small island of Baracho and soon found themselves struggling with the sails and battling gale force winds. This was only the prelude to a violent hurricane. After two days of churning seas, with monstrous black waves sweeping continually over the deck, the storm threw the ship on the reefs of a small island near the bay of Honduras. Vane's sloop staved to pieces, and the entire crew drowned. Not until much later would the fate of Deal's ship be learned. When the fury of the seas abated, Vane was found by a fisherman, who at first thought he was dead. Superstitious, the man abandoned him, and it was not until several hours later, when some saw the sodden, bruised figure on the beach begin to stir, that other fishermen carried him into a hut.

Weeks passed while Captain Vane recovered. Taken care of through the kindness of the natives, he lived on the island, catching fish and turtles for food as they did. The captain congratulated himself on his luck. Humility or thankfulness was not in his character, for he had a picture of himself as invincible. As a muddied peacock spreads his tailfeathers and begins to strut about as soon as he is dry and clean, so did Captain Vane. He stopped fishing for his own food and had the fishermen pay homage to him in the form of offerings of fish and fruit.

Finally a ship was seen on the horizon, and the captain prepared to leave. He immediately ordered some of the natives to get to work gathering dried fish and fruit for him to take on board as his own personal cache of food. The ship anchored, and one of the seamen was tying her when Vane reached the wharf. In a hearty voice, he hailed the fellow.

"How long do ye plan to be in port?"

"Only long enough for water," answered the seaman, looking over at his ship. "Eh, captain?"

"That's right," a voice said from the deck.

When Vane looked up to see the captain, he found himself staring into the eyes of the man he had once planned to murder: Captain Holford.

"Well, if it isn't my old friend, Holford," Vane said, recovering himself quickly. "Come ashore, mon. We'll have a drink and I will tell you how I happen to be here."

The two men quaffed ale together, and all the while, Vane tried his best to get Holford to take him off the island.

"Nay, Charles, I wouldn't trust you on board unless you went as a prisoner, for you would soon be plotting with my men to knock me in the head and go off pirating with my ship."

"Oh, but you shall have my word of honor as a gentleman—my most sacred oath!"

Holford was not impressed. He had no confidence in Captain Vane's promises or oaths.

"You might get off this island easily if you really wanted to," Holford suggested casually.

"And how would that be?"

"Aren't there any fisherman's boats? You could take one of them."

"Would you have me steal?"

"My eyeballs, man! Would it hurt your conscience to steal a dory when you have stolen ships and cargoes, murdered crews, plundered whenever you could!" Vane was silent and couldn't meet Holford's gaze.

"You are certainly squeamish for such a rascal, Vane. Well, I'm sailing on down the bay and will be back this way in about a month. If I find you on the island when I return, I'll think about taking you with me."

Not long after Holford's departure, another ship, on her homeward journey, put in for water and repairs at the island. Vane immediately applied to be hired and was taken on. None of the company knew him, and Vane felt safe from punishment for his crimes. He began to make friends with the crew, and soon he was seeking out malcontents who might join him in a plot should the occasion arise.

About a month later, Captain Holford returned from the bay, and, being good friends with the captain of Vane's new ship, he was invited to dine on shipboard. As he passed along to the cabin, he happened to look down in the hold, and whom should he see but the treacherous Charles Vane, hard at work.

"Do you know whom you have aboard?" he asked the captain.

"Why, only one new man, whom I shipped on at an island. A poor fellow who was cast away in a trading sloop. He seems an energetic sort."

"He is Captain Vane, the notorious pirate."

"If it is he," cried out the other, "he must leave. I won't keep him."

"I'll send for him, take him aboard and surrender him at Jamaica," said Holford, solving the shocked master's problem. As soon as

Holford returned to his ship, he sent his first mate, armed, who leveled his pistol at Vane and took him prisoner.

Word spread among Holford's crew that this man who had been serving among them was the famous pirate Captain Charles Vane, and the crew gathered at the rail, watching silently as Vane, with the mate's gun on him, descended into the small boat where two other seamen waited. As soon as the pirate was brought aboard, Holford put him in irons and took every precaution to be sure that he could not escape.

Arriving at Jamaica, Captain Holford delivered up Vane to justice. Governor Spotswood of Virginia claimed jurisdiction over the pirate, but the Jamaica court, not bothering to return him, proceeded to try him. During the trial, Vane learned that his former mate, Robert Deal, had been picked up by a man-of-war after the fateful storm, only to be hanged for piracy some months before Vane's capture.

Captain Charles Vane, who once terrorized the entire city of Charles Towne, made a desperate plea for his life before the admiralty court at Port Royal.

But the charges were lengthy, dating back two years, to 1718. Among the charges against Vane were the seizing of the *John and Elizabeth*, going from St. Augustine, Florida, to Providence, Rhode Island, with several hundred Spanish pieces of eight and its cargo; the piracy off the coast of Virginia over which Spotswood claimed jurisdiction; the capture of the *Endeavour*, six miles from Long Island; and at least four others. To all of this Vane pleaded, "Not guilty."

Witnesses were then called, some masters of the ships he had taken, and the evidence against him was overwhelming. When the court came out from behind closed doors they pronounced him guilty of piracy, and when Vane had nothing to say, their sentence resounded through the courtroom:

That he should go to the Place from whence he came, and from thence, to a place of Execution where he [is] to be Hanged by the neck, 'till he [is] dead and the Lord have Mercy upon his Soul.

On March 29, 1720, Captain Charles Vane was taken to Gallows Point and hanged. Afterward his body was hung on a gibbet, a post with a crosspiece forming a T from which infamous executed criminals were suspended by chains, so that the public could view and ridicule them.

Charles Vane was a man who betrayed every friend he ever had, and finally, it was the death of him.

Thomas Pound
New England

S hortly before midnight on Thursday, August 8, 1689, six men and a boy came down to the water's edge not far from the Bull Tavern and boarded a two-masted, half-decked fishing boat anchored at Bull's Wharf.

The leader of the group was Thomas Pound, former pilot of the king's frigate *Rose*. During the townspeople's recent insurrection against Governor Andros the Bostonians had seized the captain of the *Rose*, and in their anger against Andros, they had struck the English frigate's topmasts and brought her sails ashore. Pound, a member of the faction strongly supporting the governor, was fiercely resentful, but now he had something else on his mind.

It was a moonlit night, and in case some of the patrons of the Bull Tavern should come tumbling out the front door sober enough to notice the party of men, Pound's little band kept to the shadows. To the owner of the boat, Thomas Hawkins, Pound gave the command to hoist sails, and for a few minutes boat and crew were brightly illuminated. But as clouds drifted across the moon, the commander and his confederates disappeared in the darkness.

They sailed in the direction of the Castle, a building used for securing prisoners.

Pound knew the place well. It was from here that Governor Andros had escaped six nights before, and Pound wondered as he passed it whether he himself was suspected of playing a part in that escape. In any event all had been for naught. The governor was recaptured by the insurrectionists two days later in Rhode Island, and even at that moment was being brought back to Boston. With his fate no longer secure through his ties to Governor Andros, Thomas Pound had been quick to plan the most daring venture of his life.

He had contacted Hawkins and arranged to pay him for carrying his small company of men to Nantasket. Now, with the light of a lantern piercing the darkness, he peered at Thomas Hawkins, speculating upon the sort of man he really was. He would soon know.

When the boat reached Long Island—halfway to the agreed destination—Pound ordered Hawkins to anchor. Pound gave no explanation, and here they remained until almost daylight.

"I've changed my mind about going to Nantasket," he finally said. "My party would like to go fishing."

Hawkins hauled in the anchor, and the boat was soon under sail again. They were near Lovell's Island when finally Pound heard what he had been waiting for: the sounds of a boat being launched and men's voices.

"There they are," said seaman Thomas Johnston at his elbow. Pound had referred to Johnston as "the limping privateer" since an accident had crippled him a few years before. Johnston was tough. He was also knowledgeable in the skills of privateering, or—Pound smiled to himself—piracy. For with the signing of a piece of paper called a treaty, a privateersman who had not heard of the peace could find himself engaged in piracy. Or, with a sudden declaration of war, a pirate could turn privateer and be praised as a hero!

He heard the rhythmic dip of paddles in the water, and soon a small boat carrying five men came alongside and boarded. They were all armed, and now no one made any effort to conceal the weapons.

Pound took command.

"Throw the fish casks overboard!" he ordered. "Take an easterly course beyond the Brewster Islands at the harbor's entrance."

Pound saw Hawkins hesitate. Now he would see the mettle of the man.

"My men and I have agreed to seize the first vessel we meet and then sail her to the West Indies to prey upon the French," said Pound. "Are you with us?"

Pound was not disappointed. Hawkins agreed, and Pound made him his sailing-master.

A little while later they saw a small deck-sloop about four or five leagues off the Brewster Islands. As it drew near, Pound hailed it, Hawkins bringing the boat to windward.

"Have you any mackerel and water to spare?" called out Hawkins, and he bought fish and was given several gallons of water. But he never once brought his boat alongside the sloop. The master, Captain Isaac Prince of Hull, and his fishermen noticed this evasive course. They also saw, through cracks in the deck covering of the other boat, that a number of men appeared hidden below decks. Above deck, doing his best to conceal himself, a man peered out at them, then quickly withdrew his head. Pound, the former pilot of the *Rose*, was taking care not to be recognized. The fishermen were curious.

"Where are you bound?" Captain Prince asked Hawkins.

"To Billingsgate." (Today, Wellfleet.)

"And how do you happen to be so far north?" asked Prince. He heard laughter from below deck on the fishing boat.

"It's all one to me," Hawkins' merry reply came back, and on this note the ships parted.

Reaching Boston, Captain Prince went directly to the governor and reported on the conduct of Hawkins, who he said seemed very cheerful! Hawkins's attitude and actions were not taken too seriously, perhaps because there was often drinking on the part of men at sea.

A few hours after parting company with Prince, Pound and Hawkins were near Halfway Rock when Hawkins saw a loaded fishing ketch coming in to Boston. He and Pound conferred and decided to take the vessel. Seeing their guns, Captain Alan Chard of the *Mary* surrendered.

"This boat is my prize," said Hawkins, coming aboard the ketch and pushing Chard away from the helm. "As soon as we can take a better vessel and supply her, we're going to the West Indies and plague the French."

"You'll need more men than you have," Chard told him. He recognized Hawkins, and Thomas Johnston as well.

"Oh, we expect at least forty to join us," replied Hawkins.

They had only two gallons of powder and so few bullets that they began to melt up all the lead they could find. The following night Pound set Chard and two of his men free in the fishing boat, but he took two of Chard's crew. John Darby of nearby Marblehead went voluntarily, and Pound forced a boy who was with Chard as he could speak French and they needed an interpreter.

When Chard brought the news to Salem of how he had lost his ship to piracy, the story was relayed to the governor, and a vessel manned by the Marblehead and Salem militia went out to find and surprise the pirate ketch. But the vessel soon returned to harbor, unable to report sighting a trace of Captain Chard's ship.

Meanwhile Captain Pound was on his way to Falmouth, Maine. He reached there early on a Monday morning, the ketch anchoring about four miles below the fort. The fort contained much that Pound could use, and he set about getting it. Luckily, his man from Marblehead, John Darby, knew Sylvanus Davis, commander of Fort Loyal. While Pound's men filled water casks, Darby went to talk with the commander and arouse his sympathy with false tales of misfortune.

"We have just come from Cape Sable, where we had the misfortune to be taken by a privateer," Darby said. "We've been robbed of lead and most of our bread and water, and we need a doctor. The master of our ketch, Captain Chard, has hurt his foot."

He was convincing enough that a doctor was sent out to the ketch immediately. This was part of Pound's scheme to secure a doctor for his expedition to the Indies, but the doctor declined Pound's invitation and returned to Falmouth. He told different stories about his visit to the ketch, at one moment saying that there were only a few aboard and that they were honest men, at another claiming that he saw many men on board. Afterward the doctor was often seen in conversation with various soldiers at the fort.

Meanwhile Pound and his crew remained anchored off the fort.

The commander began to consider the possibility that the crew of the ketch might be pirates, and he ordered the soldiers to keep a close watch on the side of the fort toward the water, fearful of an attack from that direction. But he was guarding against the wrong danger. His problem was to come from within the fort itself. One night when everyone was asleep the guards and sentinels robbed their soldier companions of everything but the clothes on their backs. Carrying away with them all the ammunition they could lay hands on as well as a brass gun, the deserters rowed out to the ketch.

Next morning Commander Davis was shocked to find his men gone. Since there was little wind, the ketch was still out there. Davis decided to send two soldiers in a canoe to visit Captain Pound and demand that he send the men back to the fort immediately. Pound only laughed at the commander's ridiculous request. When asked to return the food and clothing stolen from the sleeping soldiers he also refused.

Before leaving the area he helped himself to several sheep feeding on an island in the bay; then he set sail for Cape Cod. As the boat rounded the tip of Cape Cod, Pound's eye lighted upon a fine sloop at anchor under Race Point. It was the *Good Speed*. John Smart was the master, and she was owned by David Larkin of Piscataqua. Pound and his men took possession of her, and since the *Good Speed* was a much larger vessel than Captain Chard's ketch, the pirates moved their gear and booty over to her. Smart and his men were set free and instructed to take the ketch back to Boston.

"Tell the governor that we know he has a sloop ready to send out after us," said Captain Pound, "and if she comes up with us, they'll find hot work. Every man of us will die before we will be taken."

When Smart reached Boston with this audacious message, an order was given to send out the *Resolution* commanded by Joseph Thaxter, man it with 40 seamen and seize all pirates, particularly the ones named Thomas Hawkins and Captain Pound and their associates. They were advised to be "careful in the shedding of blood unless you be necessitated by resistance. . . ."

Captain Thaxter had no more success in finding the pirates than the last expedition—probably because Captain Pound, after he had finished capturing another ship, met with a stiff northeaster and, sailing before it, was forced down the coast to Virginia, where he found his way into the York River. But he arrived at the best possible moment for a pirate evading capture. The man-of-war which was kept there had recently sunk, and the station ship was on her side being careened.

Easterly winds forced Pound and Hawkins to anchor here for a week. When the winds abated they made their way into the mouth of the James River, where they ran aground. It was a day before they could get their vessel afloat. The weather turning moderate, they sailed out of the bay unscathed and made directly for the Massachusetts coast.

Arriving at Cape Cod, the crew went ashore. After a time the men came back to the ship, but Hawkins did not return. Captain Pound did not seem distressed by his desertion. He continued happily robbing vessels off the cape, which he found an excellent place to intercept his victims.

During the latter part of September 1689, Pound sighted the *Brothers Adventure* of New London, Connecticut. Since the vessel had been forced in by bad weather, Pound induced her master, John Pickett, to anchor beside him—"for the sake of companionship" was his excuse. That night Pound and his men boarded Pickett's ship. Her cargo was just what he had been looking for—all the provisions needed for his southern voyage, including pork, beef, Indian corn, butter and cheese.

Before leaving the area Pound decided to anchor in Tarpaulin Cove and overhaul the rigging so they would be shipshape for the voyage to Curacao, the Dutch colony near the South American coast. There he would refit her before going out to loot French ships from Martinique. Pound and his men lay over in Tarpaulin Cove for two days to complete their work and were ready to leave when a sloop appeared and steered straight toward them. Pound sailed away with the sloop in swift pursuit.

It was the sloop *Mary*, under command of the distinguished Captain Samuel Pease, with a crew of 20 seamen. The governor and council at Boston had been warned of the presence of a pirate so that westward bound shipping might be aware of danger, and Pease had been instructed to take the pirates by surprise if possible. He learned that Pound had gone westward, and Pease found the pirates at Tarpaulin Cove as he had expected.

A fierce and lengthy battle ensued, and it was not without much bloodshed on both sides that Captain Samuel Pease and his men took the pirates—with both captains wounded and out of action. Pease, who was shot in the arm and thigh, lost much blood and died a few days later, leaving a widow and four orphans. Captain Thomas Pound had been shot in the side and arm and had to have several bones removed.

The wounded pirates were held in Boston's new stone jail which had a dungeon with walls four feet thick and—lest anyone think of escape—chains to keep them there. Ironically, whom should Pound meet in the jail but his old cohort, Hawkins, who had been held there since his desertion and subsequent capture several months before.

Captain Pound's friends tried to insure that he received the best medical attention available. While his wounds probably gave him the most pain, the loss of his booty must have concerned him even more. Not only had he lost his chance at a fortune; as evidence the booty was incriminating. The treasure he was carrying on his sloop was over 209,000 pounds.

Hawkins was tried first and found guilty. Pound and his men were tried several days later and found guilty of felony, piracy and murder. Their sentence was to "be hanged by the neck until they be dead," and the execution set for January 27 of 1690.

New England minister Cotton Mather, as was his unfailing custom, arrived to counsel and pray with Pound and the others.

Strangely enough, Waitstill Winthrop, one of the magistrates who had tried the pirates, was not satisfied with the verdict. Immediately after the trial Winthrop began trying to obtain a reprieve for Pound and his men, going about to request the signatures of influential people. He called on the old governor, asking that Pound be reprieved. On February 24, 1690, Pound was reprieved—thanks to the final intervention of a Mr. Epaphraa Shrimpton and several "women of quality." Thomas Hawkins's sisters had married prominent men, and their husbands' influence also played a part in both Hawkins's and Pound's respective escapes from the gallows.

Hawkins's sentence was remitted, and that of Captain Pound was temporarily delayed pending his coming trip to England, where the piracy charge would be decided.

The *Rose*, which Pound had originally piloted, had been returned to him on order of the king—perhaps due to the influence of Andros—and Captain Pound and Hawkins set out for England. En route they were attacked by a 30-gun French privateer, which they managed to outfight and outsail in a bloody battle. Thomas Hawkins was among the slain.

With his usual good luck, Captain Pound reached England safely. There he wrote to his friend Sir Edmund Andros, then in London, announcing his return. He also sent along the latest news from New England along with a short account of the fight with the privateer. A testimonial to the advantages of friends in high places was that the piracy charge was at once dismissed, and Thomas Pound was appointed captain of the frigate *Sally Rose* of the Royal Navy. Thus was virtue rewarded by his country. He and his new ship were stationed at Virginia under his old patron, Governor Andros.

But the excitement of recent years must have taken its toll upon the good captain, for in 1699 he retired to live the life of a country squire at Isleworth, England. He died there in 1703, honored and respected by all.

And this is the story of Thomas Pound, pilot of the king's frigate, who became a pirate and died a gentleman.

"Calico Jack" Rackham
New York to Florida to West Indies

"We've got hands enough for two ships," quartermaster John Rackham said to Captain Charles Vane.

They had captured two ships and their crews, and the second, a well-built vessel named the *Kingston*, had a rich cargo. It had already been fairly divided. Now Vane and Rackham—two friends who had sailed together a long time—were amiably discussing their next move. Who would have believed that within a few hours they would be at each other's throats?

"Let's divide the crew—put some of the men on the *Kingston*," suggested Vane, and Rackham nodded agreement. "Calico Jack," as everyone called him—because of the colorful calico shirt and britches he effected—was not the best fighter, but he was well liked by the men. In fact, a few hours later the crew chosen to man the *Kingston* unanimously elected John Rackham as their captain. Accord between Vane and his protege did not last an hour.

Discovering that his vessel was out of liquor, Vane sent a request for a supply to the new captain, but when it arrived he did not consider it enough. He hastened over to Rackham's ship, and in a manner that indicated he still viewed Calico Jack as his subordinate, demanded that Rackham send over more liquor. Angered, Rackham ordered him off the ship. Vane did not move.

"I'll shoot you through the head if you don't get back aboard your ship," threatened Rackham. He meant business. "Sheer off and go your own way before I sink you."

Vane stared furiously back. Then, the *Kingston* being the larger and stronger of the two ships, Vane decided to take Rackham seriously—for the moment. The two captains parted.

Rackham, who had seen Vane's fearlessness while serving under him off the Carolina coast, was proud of himself. For the first time in his career, he, Calico Jack, was showing an awesome man he had met his match. In command of his own vessel, he gave orders to head for the Island of Princes.

Not long afterward they saw an approaching sloop, and Rackham sent a boat to bring the master over for him to question.

"What's the news in the islands?" he inquired.

"War with Spain's the latest," said the master importantly as he savored Rackham's fine brandy on his tongue. The pirates crowded around and everyone began talking animatedly.

"'Twas proclaimed in Jamaica just before I left," the master continued, "and ships are already . . ."

But Rackham interrupted him. "What about a pardon for pirates? Has the time limit for surrender expired?"

"No, 'tis not yet expired—and they'll need good men for privateering."

Learning that vessels would be sent out to seize and loot Spanish ships, and that they themselves might participate in these benefits of war, the seamen were greatly excited. Rackham ordered some of his crew on an errand below deck, and they returned with several presents for the master, who began to relax a little. He had been trying to conceal his fright, for he had expected both himself and his vessel to be seized—but now he was receiving presents! A surprising turn of events. Then he learned why. The pirate captain wanted him to act as an emissary.

Calico Jack directed the master to sail back immediately to Jamaica and let the governor know they were willing to surrender provided he would give his word they would all be pardoned. They had run defiantly away from a pardon at Providence and now were not so certain of the governor's response. Rackham asked the master to return with a reply, promising to reward him well for his trouble.

Neither the master nor Rackham was prepared for the situation in Jamaica. On delivering his message, the master discovered that the former master of the *Kingston* had gotten there first and told the governor that Vane and Rackham had taken his ship. At that very moment two sloops were being readied to pursue Vane and his former quartermaster, and his Excellency was only too glad to know where the buccaneers could be found.

When the sloops arrived at the location they took Captain Rackham by surprise. In a state of complete disorganization, he was unprepared either to flee or to fight. The pirates had used the sails to erect tents along the shoreline, the decks of the ship were strewn with cargo, and most of the men were drinking and singing on shore. Calico Jack, aboard ship, saw the approach of the two sloops through his glasses and realized they were ready to attack him. He had not expected an enemy, and while he puzzled over the situation, the sloops came within firing range. There was no time or means to defend the *Kingston*. The pirate chieftain and a few hands aboard ship ran for a boat and made for shore. In his hurry Rackham left behind two women prisoners, detained from the time of the *Kingston*'s capture, to be taken by his pursuers.

Calico Jack and his men scurried to hide themselves on the uninhabited island where they could not be observed from the sea. They had some small arms but only a little ammunition, and the bales of silk stockings and boxes of lace hats they had rowed ashore before the sloops arrived were of no use in their present predicament.

Finding the *Kingston* but not the pirates, the English sloops rescued the unfortunate women and returned to Jamaica. Here the real master of the *Kingston* checked his ship and discovered 60 gold watches, packed among some bale goods, which had gone unnoticed. To his surprise, a substantial amount of the original cargo was still aboard. He confirmed, however, that a box of silver watches had been opened and pilfered by Rackham's crew.

With the *Kingston* gone Rackham possessed just two small boats and a canoe. He and a half-dozen men decided to leave for Jamaica and throw themselves upon the mercy of the governor. Other crew members disagreed, regarding Rackham with contempt and not wishing to trust to the "governor's mercy," but he decided to claim they had been abducted by Vane against their will. At this there was laughter from his men, but some changed their mind and went along.

Putting provisions and arms into the best boat—with the hope that fate might send a better one their way en route—they set sail. On the north side of Cuba their hopes were rewarded. Several Spanish ships hove into view. After a few shots, a stout sea boat surrendered, and they shifted their cargo into her.

Reaching the island of Providence in mid–May of 1719, Rackham and his men landed safely. It all went more easily than he expected. The governor saw fit to give them the king's pardon—perhaps because they were sailing a Spanish vessel, or perhaps because they had goods to sell and money to spend. After their spree was over and their funds exhausted, many of the pirate crew shipped out—some on privateers, others on trading vessels—but Captain Rackham, possessing the largest share of the booty, stayed on. It was a mistake.

His problems at Providence began with his first sight of a beautiful girl from Carolina. Red-headed, high-spirited, and strikingly lovely, her name was Anne Bonny. She might have intimidated some men, but not Calico Jack. He gave her extravagant presents to show his love, and she soon began to return it. The chief obstacle to their happiness was that Anne Bonny was married.

Her husband, James Bonny, angrily refused her request for a divorce. Once a pirate himself, he now lived on bounties from the governor for turning in his old friends. Anne thought him despicable and told Rackham so. She spoke with contempt of her husband's cowardice, and indeed James Bonny proved her right. Instead of confronting Rackham, he hurried to the governor asking him to enforce a law—seldom used even in that day—to publicly beat Anne for betraying him.

By this time Calico Jack and his mistress were already plotting to seize a fine sloop they had seen in the harbor, then leave the island by night. Rackham had begun recruiting from his onetime crew. It was not hard to find pirates weary of shore-life who longed for their old trade.

The sloop that they planned to make off with was between 30 and 40 tons and one of the swiftest sailers ever built. She belonged to a clever rogue named John Haman, and so swift was he at leaving the site after he had pillaged or plundered the Spaniards that a saying sprang up: "There goes John Haman, catch him if you can."

Following Rackham's instructions, Anne walked along the waterfront each day. Whenever she knew Haman was away, she would stop by his ship, pretending to wish to see to him. She would ask his men questions: How many of you stay on board? What sort of voyages do you make? What kind of watch do you keep? On learning that there were only two hands on board and that Haman slept ashore at night, she asked her final innocent question: "And where does each of you sleep?"

The two crewmen willingly answered, never thinking that the information they gave was being relayed to pirate Jack Rackham.

By now Rackham had engaged eight men. When he heard the governor was ready to have Anne flogged, he decided they must speed up their plan. The night they chose was dark and rainy, but the boat they planned to seize was near shore and the darkness to their advantage. He and Anne and the crew—all well armed—rowed out to Haman's boat, and when they boarded, Anne, followed by one of the men, drew her sword and pistol. She headed straight for the cabin where the two crew members slept and found them just waking up at the sound of the noise.

"If you resist, I'll blow your brains out," she warned, pointing the pistol at them levelly, and the pair saw she meant it. She and her male companion secured their prisoners' wrists and ankles. Meanwhile Rackham and his men were heaving in the cables. Freeing the sloop, they sailed down the harbor until they were opposite the fort.

"Where are you going?" voices shouted almost simultaneously from both the fort and the guard ship.

"Our cables have broken and we have nothing aboard but a grappling hook that won't hold us," Rackham called back. Setting a small sail to steer them, he then guided the ship into the harbor mouth, where the darkness swallowed it, concealing it from view of both the fort and the harbor. He quickly hoisted all the sail they had and stood to sea.

Then he called the two prisoners before him.

"Will you two gentlemen join us?" he asked, but the pair declined, and he gave them a small boat to row themselves to shore.

"Give Haman a message from me. Tell him Calico Jack Rackham will send him his sloop when he is through with her," he called down to them, flashing Anne the teasing, devil-may-care smile that he knew she found engaging.

Once at sea on the *Curlew*, Captain Rackham and his sweetheart began their loving and their piracies with a vengeance. They fought and plundered ships throughout the West Indies—until Anne became pregnant. Calico Jack suggested they go to Cuba, where many of the pirates' families lived, so she could have the baby. After the baby was born, Rackham became more and more restless. He saw Anne as a partner in his life at sea and a mistress. She began to agree. They had heard on the island of a better place to go than the Indies. Pirates—at least 2,000 by now—were terrorizing shipping off the North American coast, and many found the isolated Carolina inlets and Carolina's friendly governor, Charles Eden, to their liking. Giving up the baby to the care of a family in Cuba, Rackham and Anne set sail for Carolina.

Captain Rackham and Anne were happy except for his fits of jealousy, and these began to occur more frequently after a new member joined the crew. A slim young man with dark hair and long-lashed blue eyes, he was seen more and more with Anne. Sometimes the two would walk the deck arm-in-arm, so absorbed in conversation that Anne would not even hear Rackham if he spoke. Now he became insanely jealous.

One day after Calico Jack had flown into one of his frequent storms of accusation, Anne brought her friend to his cabin and closed the door. When they left, all was well, for Rackham now knew that this crew member was not a man but a woman. Anne was simply enjoying having the companionship of a member of her own sex on board. Her name was Mary Read—an English girl who, to escape her unhappy family life, had gone to sea in the only manner open at that time to a woman. Slim, boyish, she dressed as a man and no one was the wiser. Her secret was not revealed aboard the *Curlew* until she married a member of the crew who had been forced into piracy. Later she took his place in a duel, saving his life.

It was about the time of the duel that Anne discovered she was pregnant again.

"And what are we going to do with another baby?" Rackham asked angrily. "We will have to take this child to Cuba too!" She was deeply hurt. She knew then she would not be able to keep her second child either.

One morning as the *Curlew* sailed near Jamaica, the ship was unexpectedly attacked by a British sloop. As Anne and Mary Read fought bravely, Rackham suddenly hurried below, several crewmen following him.

"We need ammunition!" he shouted in answer to Anne's glare at him, and then he was gone.

Anne, Mary Read and one crewman continued their desperate fight, far outnumbered. Neither captain nor men ventured above. Finally Anne shouted derisively down from the entrance hatch: "You bunch of cowards—get up here and fight!"

When they gave no response, her voice came again, urgent and frightened: "Jack! Either we run them through or we'll hang."

Finally, the women surrendered. Whether Rackham and his men had been over-indulging in spirits or Rackham had turned coward, no one ever knew. Despite Anne's effort to shame them and the example of the women's fierce courage, the men had fought poorly. The *Curlew* was captured and brought into Jamaica, where all on board were jailed at Port Royal awaiting trial.

It was November of 1720 when Calico Jack Rackham, still wearing his striped pants and calico shirt, was convicted and the judge condemned him to be hanged. On the morning set for his execution at Gallows Point the captain, a shadow of his former dashing self, was permitted to visit his sweetheart, Anne Bonny. The visit was far from comforting. As he started toward her, arms raised to touch her through the bars that separated them, she coldly turned away.

"I'll never see my child," said he.

"You might have thought of that before," Anne snapped back.

And then her next words whirred through the air like the blade of a cutlass.

"I'm sorry to see this happen," said Anne, "but if you had fought like a man, you would not now be hanged like a dog!" He cringed at her words.

As the guards led Rackham away, all he could feel was the contempt of Anne's gaze which he knew followed him. It was the end of a passionate romance—and the end of Calico Jack.

Samuel Bellamy
New England to Pennsylvania
to Virginia to West Indies

The *Whydah*'s voyage north to Virginia started with fine weather and a favorable wind, but before night Captain Samuel Bellamy was to experience the strangest phenomenon he had ever witnessed at sea.

Just after sunset a spurt of fire appeared on top of the mast, and with it came a sharp sound like steam escaping from a great kettle. The flame lasted perhaps no longer than ten minutes, but clusters of amazed pirates gathered to stare upward.

"What is it?" Bellamy asked, and no one answered.

Finally the pilot spoke. "A warning, sir. Before night we shall have a dangerous storm."

"We should head for shore now," muttered one of the men.

The Indian pilot, John Julian, was respected by the crew, who believed that he had the power to foresee events—even the power to cause the wind to rise when a ship was becalmed. But Bellamy had little faith in omens, and, rather than turning back to shore, he only smiled as at a joke.

A few hours later rain blew in from the sea, and while rivulets of water streamed down the creases of his face, the captain stood laughing and shouting blasphemies to the sky. Julian watched, his dark eyes filled with fear and horror.

"Where are we?" the captain bellowed to the pilot.

"Somewhere off the Virginia Capes," came the reply.

As the breeze rose to a hard gale, the *Whydah's* crew hastened about the ship, engaged in the tasks they performed automatically when a storm was on the way. Jagged streaks of lightning pierced the darkness around them, each followed by a roll of thunder.

"Let's return the salutes of the gods," shouted Captain Bellamy defiantly. "Man the guns, men! The gods are drunk over their tipple!"

The seamen cringed at his blasphemies.

Crew member Tom Davis was convinced that neither God nor man ever frightened this captain, who was often bold to the point of recklessness. Would he bring disaster upon them all?

His mind traveled back to the story Bellamy told of beginning his pirate career in the town of Nassau on New Providence Island, tutored by the notorious Captain Benjamin Hornigold. There came a time when for weeks they met no Spanish ships to plunder, yet Captain Hornigold steadfastly refused to capture English vessels. The crew of the *Mary Anne* became infuriated and rebellious. They had no idea that Hornigold was wrestling with a decision of his own— whether to remain a pirate or accept the king's pardon and live out his life as an honest man.

One day, after a particularly long and heated dispute between the pirates and Hornigold, Bellamy himself lost patience and shouted boldly above the crew's angry voices.

"I call for election of a new captain!"

"Aye, aye," the men chorused, and when the vote to oust Hornigold was counted, it was 90 to 26. Bellamy was a natural leader, a man of persuasive oratory with no scruples about seizing the ships of any country, and the crew immediately voted him in as captain.

Generously presenting his former mentor with a prize sloop, Bellamy watched one of the most famous pirates of his day sail back toward New Providence Island to renounce his way of life forever.

Now in charge of about 90 pirates—most of them English—Bellamy took his first prize. It was the *Sultana*, a man-of-war. She was commanded by Captain James Richards, and while she was certainly not the ship of his dreams, she was faster and better appointed than the *Mary Anne*. He moved over to the *Sultana*, making her command ship of his four-vessel pirate flotilla.

But in late February 1717 Bellamy sighted a real ship, new and magnificent—the most impressive he had ever seen. A ship-rigged galley about 100 feet in length, she was named for an African port, *Whydah*. Some African port towns were known for their trade in ivory or gold; Whydah was known for slave trade, and it was for that purpose that the ship had been designed. To give her extra speed she was equipped with oar holes and sweeps on the lower deck so that oars could be manned by the crew if the ship was becalmed.

Bellamy saw her speed and versatility as ideal for his "life on account" (as pirates called their profession). Drawing close, he lofted the *Sultana*'s grim death's head ensign. Most vessels would have immediately capitulated, fearing cruel treatment if they resisted. But the *Whydah*, to the amazement of Bellamy's crew, did not surrender. Instead, the captain, aware that his precious cargo was in jeopardy, led them a brave chase, and for three days Bellamy pursued, with the *Whydah* outsailing and outrunning his vessel.

At last the wind favored the pirates. Now, league by league, they began to gain upon their victim, and on the east side of Long Island, in the Bahamas, they caught her. Even then, the *Whydah*'s brave captain made one last defiant gesture, firing two guns at the pirates, but he knew when he had been bested, and he followed the gunfire by striking his colors.

Laurence Prince, commander of the *Whydah*, had done everything possible to resist the pirates. Now his crew waited apprehensively to learn their fate.

Bellamy swung aboard, a fearsome sight with his great head sporting an unruly mop of jet hair. He flourished a bare cutlass, and a brace of elaborately decorated pistols glittered ominously in the silk sash wound about his waist. "I am the Robin Hood of the seas," he shouted. All aboard the *Whydah* stood motionless, awaiting the pirate's commands. But to their surprise, out of a deep respect for Commander Prince's courageous effort to escape, Bellamy wreaked no punishment upon commander or crew. At a signal from him his men simply began to go through the cargo. It was, indeed, a rich haul. The ship was carrying 20,000 to 30,000 English pounds sterling. The actual weight of the gold and silver she carried may have amounted to as much as 9,000 pounds.

Soon Bellamy was treating Commander Prince more as a friend than an adversary, confiding in him on personal matters. He even told Prince about Maria Hallett, a girl with whom he had fallen in love on a trip to Cape Cod the year before.

As for himself, Prince was eager to continue on to England.

"Take the *Sultana*," the pirate captain said generously with a wave of his hand at his former ship. "I wish you a good voyage to London, captain."

Bellamy's pleasure over acquiring the *Whydah* was such that he did not mind sharing booty, and he loaded the English commander down with some of the finest goods. Tom Davis saw him push a heavy purse filled with gold and silver across the table to Prince. He was coming to respect, sometimes even like, Bellamy.

Sailors on legitimate vessels were poorly paid and brutally treated, so it is not surprising that several of Prince's crew volunteered to join Bellamy. Perhaps they envied the democracy on board a pirate ship that existed nowhere else, for every buccaneer had an equal vote on decisions of importance, and multi-racial pirate crews all worked together as equals. Despite his generosity, Bellamy was not above forcing three good seamen to join him, including Commander Prince's boatswain. Bellamy's crew was now about 130 fighting men. He felt ready to out-race and out-fight any vessel afloat.

"It won't be long before I return to New England and my sweetheart," seaman Tom Davis later remembered Captain Bellamy saying to Prince. "And I'm not going back to her empty-handed."

It seemed to Bellamy then that neither he nor the crew would return without a vast amount of treasure. The *Whydah* was now carrying gold, silver and rich cargo from over 40 ships, and more vessels would be captured before she finally reached Cape Cod.

Tom Davis remembered those early days on the *Whydah*, but had little time to reflect on the past once the storm was fully upon them. For four days, he and the rest of the crew fought its savagery. Sharp reports of the sails tearing to pieces in the tempest were like the sounds of battle. The main topsail was split to threads, her yard bending so that the lower mast whipped about like a reed. Then the hull began to leak, and the captain, wet to the skin, strove with the storm. Above the raging of the wind, Bellamy could sometimes be heard cursing the fearful and encouraging the brave.

The winds were west by north and so fierce that had they been easterly they would have dashed the *Whydah* upon the coast. With tackles attached to the gooseneck of the tiller, it was all that four men in the gunroom and Bellamy and his pilot at the wheel could do to keep her head to the sea. Had she once broached to, the ship would have foundered.

The *Whydah* scudded all night long under bare poles, and at daybreak they were forced to cut away the mainmast, sprung in the step. At the same moment the mizzenmast fell. Bellamy saw it go, and the ship rang with his curses. His oaths increased when they tried the pumps. The *Whydah* was taking on water, and the lee pump could barely keep the water from gaining, although the men kept it going continually. By now the ship was at the mercy of the storm.

Breaking upon the poop, the sea drove in the taffarel and washed two men from the wheel. They were saved in the netting, Bellamy himself helping to rescue them. One was John Julian, who went back to the wheel without a word. The captain drove his battered and exhausted crew as the storm raged for four days and three nights. At last the wind's fury abated, fixing north by northeast. The weather was clearing.

Jury-masts were set up, and carpenter Tom Davis found the leak in the bows, which he repaired with oakum working out of a scam. The sloop had received no other damage apart from the loss of the mainsail, which the first gust had torn away from the boom. The crew became cheerful once more.

Now the wind changed, coming from the south, and Bellamy made his fateful decision to press on to New England—perhaps based on his promise to Maria Hallett that he would return. For the first time, the idea of marriage had entered his head.

On his way north, Bellamy harassed shipping lanes from Virginia to Massachusetts, and with her 28 cannons the *Whydah* was a formidable sight bearing down on her prey.

Bellamy's reputation for rhetoric, is exemplified in his conversation with a captain Beer from Boston. Beer's ship was one captured on the way to Massachusetts, and the captain was put aboard the *Whydah* while the pirates plundered the vessel.

Following the robbery, Bellamy and officer Paul Williams were for returning the ship to Beer, but the crew wanted to sink her, for they were convinced that the return of the plundered ship to port could provide evidence to hang them. "Sink her," was the vote of the majority, and Bellamy expressed his regret with characteristic eloquence:

> I am sorry they won't let you have your sloop again for I scorn to do any one a mischief, when it is not for my advantage;—the sloop, we must sink her, and she might be of use to you. Though you are a sneaking puppy, and so are all those who will submit to be governed by laws which rich men have made for their own security; for the cowardly whelps have not the courage otherwise to defend what they get by their knavery; but —ye altogether; — them for a pack of crafty rascals, and you, who serve them, for a parcel of hen-hearted numskulls. They vilify us, the scoundrels do, when there is only this difference, they rob the poor under cover of the law forsooth, and we plunder the rich under the

protection of our own courage. Had you not better make one of us, than sneak after these villains for employment?

Captain Beer replied that his conscience would not allow him to break the laws of God and man, to which Bellamy responded:

You have a devilish rascal of a conscience! I am a free prince, and I have as much authority to make war on the whole world as he who has a hundred sail of ships at sea, and an army of 100,000 men in the field; and this my conscience tells me: but there is no arguing with such snivelling puppies who allow superiors to kick them about deck at pleasure.

For Bellamy piracy was a business, and he had no taste for wanton destruction, but he abided by the vote of the majority. After sinking Captain Beer's ship, he put him ashore on Block Island.

Capturing the *Mary Anne* of Cape Cod, a vessel laden with wine, Bellamy placed seven of his men aboard the prize under Williams, his quartermaster, with orders to stay near the *Whydah*. They left Thomas Baker, captain of the wine ship, on board with the pirates. Near midday on April 26 they sighted the *Mary Anne* of Dublin, a yellow and blue sloop mounting eight guns, between Nantasket and New York. Captain Andrew Crumpstey, her master, struck his colors and surrendered when the first puff of smoke floated, up from the galley's gun tier.

" 'Tis a good start this early in the day," said Bellamy with satisfaction, and he sent a prize crew of seven pirates aboard, ordering Crumpstey to bring his cargo papers and five crewmen to the *Whydah*. Williams, meanwhile, began sailing Baker's ship northward. Bellamy's crew, elated over news of Baker's cargo of wine, sent a second boat to follow Williams, but once aboard the ship they could not get into the hold. First they hoisted a boat off the hatches, then the hatches had to be opened, and then they found the ship's cable lying in a great coil blocking the hatchway. Discouraged, the pirates finally removed five bottles of green wine from the galley and took them back to the *Whydah* for a celebration—not much of a party, for Williams' ship sailed on and became separated from them. Williams and Bellamy were not destined to meet again.

On the fateful night of April 26, the fleet consisted of the *Whydah*, the *Anne Galley* commanded by pirate Richard Noland, and the *Mary Anne* of Dublin. Sailing north-northwest for several hours in the late afternoon, they entered a thick fog, and as they did they met the *Fisher*—a sloop they took with no resistance. Commanded by Captain Robert Ingols, the *Fisher* was on its way to Boston from Virginia, carrying Virginia tobacco, hides and other merchandise.

"Do you know this coast?" Bellamy asked Ingols.

"I know it well," he replied.

Bellamy then ordered him, along with his first mate, aboard the *Whydah* to join his own advisers on the best way to navigate the cape. His collection of advisers also included Captain Crumpstey from the *Mary Anne* of Dublin, a pirate named Lambert, and John Julian. Julian was a Cape Cod native. Holding a conference, they decided that they were only a few leagues off the cape. The fog was now so thick that even approaching night could not make matters any worse. Bellamy ordered that lights be placed on the stern of each ship to help the other vessels keep their bearings, and the consensus was to cautiously sail the *Whydah* north.

At ten o'clock that night a heavy rain began to fall, accompanied by thunder and lightning. The captured *Fisher*, with four pirates aboard, lost sight of the *Whydah*'s light and mistakenly followed the *Anne Galley*. The *Mary Anne*'s mate did not realize how near shore she was until she was among the breakers, and before he could trim the head sails and come about the vessel drove aground behind Stage Harbor.

Ten miles to the north, Bellamy sensed the *Whydah*'s course was all wrong, but he was still confident he could ride out the storm.

"We must wear her around," he ordered the pilot.

"Aye, aye, sir. And her head?"

"North-northwest like she was before she broke off."

Suddenly Bellamy heard the thunder of the surf and knew the ship's head was almost on the breakers. He dropped anchor to avoid being driven upon the sand bars by the gale, but the *Whydah* was soon at the end of her cable. She began to pull her anchors—one of which weighed at least half a ton. Giving first consideration to the lives of his men, Captain Bellamy ordered the cables cut. He would try to maneuver the vessel back to sea.

"Luff all you can," he shouted, and then his voice thundered: "There's no room to wear! I'm going to club haul her. Off to your stations for tacking."

The stricken *Whydah* was thrashing furiously like a wounded whale in the midst of the foaming sea. She was now only a quarter of a mile from the beach. Bellamy signaled to put down the helm. He cut away the bower anchor.

"Haul! Haul!" he shouted, flinging the words desperately into the gale as the yards spun around and wind caught at the sails. For just a moment she was on an even keel. He gave a roaring, exultant laugh. They would make it!

Then came a terrible grinding sound and a thud that shook the *Whydah's* entire length. The cable upon which he relied to hold the ship away from the shore was holding her fast on the shoals instead. Darkness and fog made it impossible for him to see the water. The last sound Samuel Bellamy heard was the raging sea striking the starboard bow, blow after blow, an angry Neptune's fist.

Then the *Whydah* capsized, sending one man after another into the midst of waves more than 30 feet high. A few made a wild rush to the *Whydah's* hold, tried to carry their treasure with them, and drowned because of the weight of the 50-pound bags of booty. The 300-ton ship—her rigging a disordered web of tangled lines and fallen spars—tore asunder.

And the fate of the captain? He perished without seeing Maria Hallett again. He would never know that she had given birth to his child, or that the harsh puritanism practiced by the villagers had sent the girl away to live alone on the dunes.

Freezing water and savage surf dispatched all but two of the 180 men on board: pilot John Julian and carpenter Tom Davis. A few days after the storm Davis was sitting in Barnstable Gaol. He would eventually be tried for piracy and acquitted. In jail he had ample time to think. The ancients would have said that his former captain had angered Neptune, god of the sea. The pious Julian believed that Captain Bellamy had mocked the Christian god once too often.

But Tom Davis, unconcerned with vengeful deities, would always think that the captain was a more decent pirate than most!

And what of the treasure that went down with the *Whydah*? Until recently, its wealth lay buried beneath the shifting sands off Cape Cod. It has intrigued more than two centuries of treasure hunters and even drawn the interest of the famous writer Thoreau.

The wreck of the *Whydah* was finally discovered by Barry Clifford, a native of Cape Cod. As a young boy he had heard the story from his uncle, and his dream was to discover the treasure. He became a diver and a salvager and spent years planning his goal. Serious work began on the project in 1978, but he did not put a boat into the water until 1983. In July of 1984 he found the first cannon and coins. To date over 100,000 artifacts and almost 10,000 coins have been recovered, but the greatest thrill for Barry Clifford was the fall of 1985 when he brought up the bell with the name *Whydah* engraved upon it. This was the confirming evidence that he had discovered the legendary pirate ship.

Clifford's expeditions in the sea off Cape Cod have resulted in the recovery of Spanish gold doubloons, the famous silver coins known as pieces-of-eight, gold beads from the west coast of Africa, gold and silver ingots, pistols, pewterware, clothing and cannons.

"Treasures of the Whydah" has been the most popular exhibit at Cape Cod's Provincetown Museum.

William Kidd
American Coast to Red Sea

It was 1695 and a confident, boisterous Scotsman, William Kidd, son of a Presbyterian minister, was catapulting his way out of the ragged, rowdy brotherhood of piracy of the Caribbean and into the favor of the British ruling class. He was learning the ways men often employ to rise in their careers and how the wealth and prestige of influential backers could make or break him in the daring venture he had conceived.

The sea was swarming with pirates who came and went, bringing in rich cargoes from the Indies, the Red Sea and other places where the methods of obtaining it were often shrugged away. It was Kidd's idea to give the buccaneers a surprise. He and his backers would outfit a ship to intercept the pirates as they returned from plundering their prey.

Rising and stretching his legs to dispel the stiffness, William Kidd glanced appreciatively around the London pub where the junto was meeting. His piercing eyes took in the ancient oak floorboards, wide as the spars of a ship, and a fire of wood and peat that crackled pleasantly in the huge stone fireplace, its leaping orange flames illumining a diverse group.

The names of the men in this enterprise could scarcely have been more impressive—Shrewsbury, Somers, Romney, Russell and the influential, if usually penniless, Lord Bellomont. The king himself had pledged 3,000 pounds of his own money to purchase a share of ten percent. And although Bellomont finally had to go to Sir Edward Harrison to borrow the money for his share of the venture, his influence was to prove invaluable.

By grant of the Great Seal of England, the partners—now listed as Bellomont, Harrison and four surrogates for the other various lords involved—were holders of a plum. They had the right to divide all booty according to shares, free of any other claims upon the spoils—namely a claim by the crown. This had been much harder to gain than the letter permitting privateering.

"To our success in gaining permission to hunt down pirate rascals," said Bellomont, raising his glass. Kidd saw that Bellomont, scion of a family that had always been close to the throne, wanted to be certain his influence received all the credit for bringing this about.

"May the pirates Tew and Ireland and Mayes beware!" said Lord Somers. They all raised their glasses again.

"Our friend, Captain Kidd, will deal with them," said Somers and he gave a somewhat haughty nod in Kidd's direction. Kidd knew that Somers looked down on him for he lacked position in society, but he was not humbled. Somers and all the others needed him to carry out this scheme every bit as much as he needed them.

The former pirate and the Earl of Bellomont, an aristocrat, were at opposite poles of the society, yet the earl thrust his arm through Kidd's as they left the pub.

"My friend, we are as different as day and night," Bellomont confessed, fatuous from the effects of too much brandy and the heat inside, "yet I have utter confidence in you." Kidd's glowing predictions had convinced these members of the peerage that he would make them all a fortune.

"I thank ye," said Kidd in a loud, hearty voice that made even the tipsy Bellomont cringe, but Kidd did not notice. He was thinking about the earl's words: "I have confidence in you."

It was just what his wife had said to him in New York before he left her to go to England, and, at her insistence, he had made her a promise. He was aware that the new life he had been leading as a businessman in New York had given him a second chance. But what new venture could be more ideally suited to him than the one he was about to undertake—to go back to sea to catch pirates when he had once been a pirate himself? Kidd chuckled at the thought.

The next day he began his search. He must find just the right vessel—spacious enough to carry plenty of fighting men, solid enough to withstand cannon barrage and small enough to careen so that he could periodically clean off the growth of barnacles and weeds that slow a ship. Careening had to be done on a beach with a steep rise, the vessel turned first on one side, then the other. Bigger ships needed a dockyard, found only in a larger port—a convenience that might not always be available to him.

Finally Kidd found just what he sought. It was the *Adventure Galley*, a vessel of 287 tons and 34 guns similar to the galley-frigates developed as patrol craft by the Royal Navy in the late 1600s. Swift, mobile, she boasted a combination of sails and oars that would make her a formidable fighting ship in tight quarters in any kind of weather. She was high-powered and three-masted with a line of oar ports along her lower deck. With three men to an oar she could do three miles an hour. It was the perfect ship to hunt pirates.

On September 6, 1696, the ship was ready to head out of the Thames into the North Atlantic. But when the *Adventure* left the dock on its voyage to America, William Kidd committed a childish act that endangered his entire enterprise. As his ship glided down the river and passed the royal yacht, Captain Kidd, with a grin in the direction of royalty, neglected to make any courtesy sign of recognition. A warning flag rang out from the royal yacht, but the *Adventure Galley*'s flags continued to flutter insolently on high.

The affront was intentional—a nose-thumbing gesture—and Kidd's crew, catching the spirit of the occasion, clambered up into the yardarms and gave an often used but rude salute. They slapped their rears in unison.

The English lords watched this without humor, and Kidd repeated the gesture a few minutes later in the direction of another ship. When this crude and reckless breach of courtesy, surprising in a man of 50 years, was shown toward the second ship, the lords were angry enough to order the *Adventure Galley* boarded, and Kidd's crew was hauled away to a naval vessel called the *Duchess*. For Kidd, the situation held the potential of dire consequences. The Royal Navy, desperate for men since France had threatened to invade England, was as apt as not to impress Kidd's entire crew. The man the king and peerage had trusted with a major venture stood humiliated at the rail of the *Adventure*, kicking himself for his buffoonery. Staring over at the *Duchess* where his men were being held, Captain Kidd could only pray that the French fleet would not invade England. If they did, his hopes for prestige and a fortune were at an end.

The captain's prayers must have been answered, for the invasion rumor was only a scare with no substance behind it—but the *Duchess* still would not release his men. Kidd had played the fool, and he must now humble himself and appeal to the Earl of Oxford for the return of his crew. His plea succeeded in getting the majority released, but the *Duchess* kept some of his best seamen, and there was nothing to do but leave England on his transatlantic trip without them.

The seamen signing on in New York looked upon the expedition as quick money, and there was no difficulty hiring a crew whom it would later be claimed were all "upright, reliable men." But practically speaking, everyone knew privateering called for strong sword arms and strong stomachs, and that they were hired on a "no prey, no pay" basis. If they failed to capture ships they would return home empty-handed.

Kidd was disturbed by the number of novices—landsmen who flocked to the city from the farms of New Jersey and Pennsylvania to sign on with him, and he stopped after recruiting 90 additional men as the ship could only hold about 150. Most of these landsmen would make poor fighters when it came to capturing pirates and would not be accustomed to the instant obedience required on a ship, where it could mean life or death. But he had found at least a core of experienced seamen, some of whom had been privateersmen or pirates themselves.

During August, barrels and boxes, fresh vegetables, dried fish and other supplies for the long journey ahead were loaded into the hold of the *Adventure*. As on most privateers, everything was governed by the amount of supplies. The ship could carry roughly two tons of provisions for the number of men on board, and the captain had to shape their course in order not to run out. It would be a long voyage from New York to the Indian Ocean and from there to their destination. Bad luck or miscalculation could easily ruin the venture.

By the end of the month the pace of the preparations grew hurried. The crew gathered briefly, and a New York City magistrate read Kidd's commission. It was time to sail in order to use the wind and weather to get to the Red Sea and avoid the winter storms of the North Atlantic. They must reach the South Atlantic during the Southern Hemisphere summer, round the Cape of Good Hope and plot their course before the southwest monsoons began in April.

And then came the day when Captain Kidd said his goodbyes to his wife and children.

"My only desire is to have you back here in New York safely, and don't forget your promise—both to me and to the king of England," cautioned the elegant blonde woman standing beside Captain Kidd on the dock on the day of his departure. "You are sworn to take pirate ships, or those that belong only to nations with whom our country of England is at war. At present that means France."

The strong face and large, commanding eyes looked down at her, and he answered tenderly and solemnly.

"You have my word for that, Sarah. How could I touch the ship of a peaceful country?"

"Perhaps I worry too much about you since I've been twice widowed. I couldn't bear it if anything ever—" He put a finger over her lips.

"I won't let anything happen—for both our sakes," he said, embracing her and pressing his face against her hair.

Sarah Bradley Cox Oort and William Kidd had been married May 16, 1691—only days after the death of her second husband. Her quick remarriage to an adventurer who had been a privateer—perhaps even a pirate!—had been the talk of New York City. It had been five years ago now but to her, he was still the most exciting man she had ever met.

"It's not just the danger you will face in attacking pirates," she went on. "There are other dangers."

"Sea monsters?"

She didn't return her husband's teasing smile. "You know."

"My beautiful lady, no man could be better suited to this particular mission than I." His eyes were merry.

"And that is just where temptation and danger lie," she warned.

"No more. My days of piracy are behind me forever," Kidd assured her, shaking his head. Then he kissed Sarah goodbye, gave a great bear hug to the two little girls who stood beside her, and boarded.

For a while Kidd's thoughts lingered on his wife, whom he adored. She had looked especially lovely on the walk together from their home on New York's Pearl Street to the dock where the *Adventure Galley* was almost ready for departure. He had been separated from her for those long months in England as he planned this venture, and now he was genuinely saddened by the knowledge that it would be at least two years before his return. Why couldn't he be happy with his new life as a successful New York businessman? He was 50 and should be glad to settle down, but the terrible restlessness—the yearning for adventure and the sea—had always seemed just beneath the surface of all his business ventures.

It was late summer of 1696 and the gray-haired, flamboyantly dressed Kidd swaggered about the quarterdeck of the *Adventure Galley*, giving orders to the crew in preparation for leaving the harbor of New York. He was in high spirits as he commanded this new and powerful ship.

Once out to sea, however, he began to think seriously about the dangerous business ahead. He needed more weapons for his seamen. It was also apparent that his backers had estimated far less than he would need in the way of cash. Any mariners on the islands, if they had money to lend, were likely to be pirates who had just returned from a successful voyage. Depending on the length of the voyage and his luck, a shortage of money could present a problem.

The Cjomoros Islands and Joanna, which would later be called Anjouan, made convenient stops for him on the way to India. At various islands the captain sent letters back to his wife filled with glowing predictions of pirate ships laden with treasure just beyond the horizon. But as the months wore on and they did not encounter any pirates to capture and plunder, fine wines, luxury items and even some staples were in short supply. The crew grew bored with their fare and restless.

Finally they reached the entrance to the Red Sea, and it was here that they sighted a heavily laden convoy of Dutch merchant ships. For a privateer from England, these ships held no promise, since England and Holland were not at war—indeed, a Dutch king sat on the English throne. But when the sun rose above the water next morning the masters of the Dutch ships discovered that a wolf was in the fold, the *Adventure Galley*, and it was flying the bloody flag.

Kidd extended a courteous invitation to the other captains to visit him on his ship, but his overtures were promptly refused. For a time he continued to sail among them, but Captain Kidd's men, meeting the seamen from the merchant ships in the bars on shore, were both disgruntled and foolish enough to confide that their captain was desperate for supplies and sails and that he hoped to separate one of the Dutch ships from the others and seize what he needed. A merchant ship bolder than the others finally fired upon the *Adventure Galley*. With its men shouting threats from the rigging, the brave Dutch vessel actually began to chase the pirate ship.

Kidd edged away, and to the surprise of the merchant convoy he sailed off. If a lucky shot should disable his ship, he would be at their mercy. No act of piracy had as yet been committed, but the threat of the red pirate flag was clear, and members of his crew who thought they had signed on for privateering were not happy to find themselves on a pirate ship. They wanted to leave. Others who were former pirates were disgusted with Kidd over his reluctance to attack cargo ships regardless of the flag they flew. The crew began to quarrel and fight with one another. Some of his men even tried to escape on a ship's boat, and about ten reached Carwar, India, where they reported Kidd's activities to the East India Company. They were happy to escape. But others, recaptured in the attempt, were forcibly brought back to the ship and flogged. As soon as the Dutch ships had returned to port they reported Kidd's raising the pirate flag in the midst of their convoy, and news of his threatening act spread.

Meanwhile Kidd still had not encountered any pirate ships laden with loot, and his frustrated men were turning ugly. Not only was there no pay, they also needed water badly.

On the Malabar Coast in August of 1697, he encountered a small English trading ship from Bombay, and in talking with its captain, Thomas Parker, who had been incautious enough to come over to the *Adventure*, Kidd professed to be surprised when he learned that he was already considered a pirate. After the report of the Dutch ships in other ports that he had appeared in their midst waving the bloody flag, the news had traveled.

While the two captains shared a bottle of rum, Kidd's deckhands boarded the trading ship and hoisted several of Captain Parker's men aloft with ropes. As the shoulders of these poor men were slowly pulled from the sockets, Kidd's crew beat them with cutlasses, shouting at them to reveal what money was hidden aboard. They finally located 100 pieces-of-eight—enough to buy a small amount of supplies—seized the food on the ship and sent Captain Parker below deck. He would be held there a long time, for he might be useful to Kidd for navigation advice, and keeping him prisoner would certainly keep news of Kidd's actions quiet.

Here on the Malabar Coast, Captain Kidd made the transition to pirate.

Whatever his intentions when he and his fellow investors planned the voyage in England, and whatever the promises he had made to Sarah, there was no retracing his steps.

On October 30, near the tip of India, the Adventure Galley lay close to an East India Company ship called the Loyal Captain. Kidd's men grew furious over his reluctance to attack it. He was maintaining a policy of not harming company ships, probably because of the East India Company's reputation for swift retaliation. As a commercial enterprise the company was a powerful enemy of piracy, had considerable influence with governments and as early as 1698 was making Kidd's name symbolic of all pirates.

Captain Kidd summoned Captain How, captain of the East India Company ship, aboard. Captain How swore that his cargo was nothing but sugar, and Kidd managed to cajole his men into leaving the ship alone.

But his crew had now turned predominantly pirate. They wanted to hold Captain How, and only by alternately threatening and making promises was Kidd able to get them to permit the captain to leave the Adventure. How was wise enough to depart quickly while Kidd was still able to control his men.

Kidd's situation was more and more precarious. He was unable to get supplies from other ships, for their captains were suspicious of him even when he offered to pay. His men had little money, and those who had once been pirates were athirst to follow their profession. Even those who ordinarily had not the temperament for it saw no reason to hold back since they had earlier raised the flag. But whether it was because of the promise he had made to his wife or his responsibility to his backers in England, Captain Kidd still deluded himself that he was not a pirate.

After How left, Kidd heard gunner William Moore on deck urging the crew on.

"Let's take How's ship!" Moore shouted to a group of men around him, and Kidd blasted him for his mutinous words.

"You lousy dog! I make the decisions," he bellowed at Moore.

"If I am a lousy dog, you have made me so; you've brought me to ruin and many more!" the gunner blazed back.

"Ruined you—you dog!" In his wrath Kidd picked up a wooden bucket and hurled it at Moore's head, and the fellow dropped to the deck, screaming an insult as he fell.

"Villain!" Kidd cried out angrily.

Moore lay in his bunk that afternoon and all night but died the next day of a fractured skull. Kidd's situation was now more dangerous by the minute, for a precedent had been set to challenge his authority. He must find a prize quickly.

But the *Adventure Galley* was still short of money and supplies. Help finally came in the shape of the *Rupparell*, a Dutch-owned vessel commanded by a Captain Michael Dickers. Kidd decided on a trick. He ordered his English flags lowered and the French colors raised as he approached. Firing several shots, he waited for her captain to come aboard, hoping that his display of the French flags would work. When Captain Dickers came into the large cabin, he encountered a Frenchman (actually serving under Kidd and pretending to be the *Adventure Galley*'s captain), who introduced himself: "I am Monsieur le Roy, captain of this ship."

Confronted by this imposter and taken in, Dickers pulled a French pass out of his pocket. It would seem that documents purporting to be from different countries were no more hard to come by than forged papers have ever been.

"By God, I've caught you. You are a free prize," cried out Kidd, who had been standing inconspicuously to one side and now stepped forward, seizing Dickers' arm.

Captain Dickers had fallen victim to an old trick, and Kidd could claim to be acting legally because his commission allowed him to seize French ships. His ship once taken over, Dickers and two of his men joined the pirates. Since Kidd's crew had taken the *Rupparell* in November, they renamed it the *November*. There was little cash on board, and as they were still short of supplies the cargo had to be turned into money as soon as possible.

Attaching the *November* to the *Adventure Galley* by a towline, the pirates continued their hunt for a bigger prize.

But the sort of good luck which would rescue their fortunes did not occur. Without incident, a month went by, and it was after Christmas in 1697 when Kidd and his men captured a small ketch. It carried coffee with enough sugar for them to sweeten it, and that was about all. Stopping the ship, they robbed it with no pretense of legality. Two weeks later they victimized a Portuguese ship. These robberies were only a matter of bread and butter, for Kidd and his men were again short of food, but they were piracy.

The long-sought "big prize," however, was on its way. On January 30, 1698, the *Quedah Merchant* began its voyage from Surat to the Spice Islands. A 400-ton ship, it carried a cargo valued between 200,000 and 400,000 rupees. The ship was in the safekeeping of an English captain named John Wright. A significant amount of the cargo had belonged to the court at Bengal, India, and having sailed there safely, the ship was on her return trip unescorted, carrying silk, calico, opium, sugar and saltpeter. As the *Quedah* rounded the southern tip of India, Kidd decided to play the same trick he had played so successfully on the *Rupparell*. Flying his French colors, he intercepted the large cargo ship. Wright, not knowing he was being tricked, put up his own set of French flags, and when he was summoned to the *Adventure Galley* he sent a Frenchman, one of his gunners, to masquerade as captain. But the man could not convince Monsieur le Roy (who always acted the part of a French captain on the *Adventure Galley*) that he was really the captain of the *Quedah*. Wright's decision to play games resulted in disaster for his vessel. Undeceived, Kidd sent for the true captain. Wright came, and his ship was claimed as a prize. Captain Wright was destined to join the long-suffering Captain Parker, whom Kidd was still holding prisoner below decks on the *Adventure Galley*.

Coji Babba, an Armenian merchant on board the *Quedah*, tried to ransom the ship itself by offering Kidd 20,000 rupees for it, but Kidd kept it. Each man on the *Adventure Galley* received 200 rupees, and tension among Kidd's crew eased.

Unfortunately the *Quedah Merchant* was no ordinary ship. It was leased out to a leading member of the emperor of India's own court and his friends. The loss of the investment not only enraged the palace, but mobs filled the streets of Surat, infuriated at yet another act of the European pirates. The East India Company stopped all trade with the English company as well as with the Dutch and French. From the standpoint of public opinion in England and the colonies, Kidd could not have chosen a worse vessel to seize.

Next he and his crew took a small Portuguese ship, adding it to their flotilla, and then started in pursuit of an East India ship, the *Sedgewick*. It flew the unmistakable East India Company flag, and this was the first time Kidd had violated his own policy and purposely tried to take a company ship. He chased it for three days, its captain, Lockyer Watts, staying just ahead of him. By the clever maneuver of letting his ship's convoy of boats tow the *Sedgewick*, Watts added considerable speed to his vessel and thus made his escape. Of course, he did not fail to report his narrow escape from Kidd when he reached safety.

At sea for almost three years, Captain Kidd perhaps began to consider the fact that the *Quedah* was slowing down and less seaworthy. He was laden with treasure—a temptation to other ships who might suspect it—and also burdened with the responsibility for getting the junto's share back to England. He must at the same time hang on to his own portion of the spoils. His friend Bellomont, coming over from England, had replaced Fletcher as governor of New York, Massachusetts Bay and New Hampshire.

Kidd had heard something of the anti-piracy sentiment back in the colonies, but he was quite unaware of his ferocious reputation in England. Each story about him had added to the growing public indignation toward buccaneers. Pirates were falling out of favor everywhere. More and more legitimate shipping firms were plying their trade back and forth to the Indies and other countries, and merchants found these companies more reliable to do business with than pirates.

Most unfortunately for him, Kidd did not know that the king had sent a proclamation to Bellomont declaring Kidd a pirate and placing the governor under a royal order to capture him.

It was approaching midnight in June of 1699 when three sloops drew alongside the large vessel lingering between Gardiner's Island and Block Island in New York waters. Mrs. Kidd, her daughters and James Emott, a loyal friend of Kidd, went aboard the large ship. Cargo, some of the passengers and crew were transferred from Kidd's vessel to the sloops. Part of this cargo was the share of the fortune Captain Kidd considered his own, and part belonged to crew members. According to later reports there was a six-pound bag of pieces-of-eight, bales of cloth, slaves, silver and gold, jewels and bags of money.

"I am sure Bellomont plans to seize you if you go to Boston," warned Kidd's wife.

"I don't think so. He will only question me, my dear."

"Why not send James Emott to talk with him before you go," the apprehensive Sarah Kidd urged.

Captain Kidd was taking precautions for his personal safety as well as the treasure. He stored his portion of it in other hands to reclaim later. Because of his wife's warnings he had become more concerned about the government's anti-piracy campaign.

He decided to write Bellomont defending himself against the stories about acts of piracy. Emott would hand-carry it. The captain sat down at the elaborate table in his large cabin and wrote out an explanation of how his men had forced him, against his will, to plunder two Moorish ships. "About 100 of my men revolted from me at Madagascar, and my life was in great danger because I refused to turn pirate," was one of the statements he made in his letter.

Because of the prominent men among Kidd's backers, himself included, Governor Bellomont decided to negotiate with the captain in order not to scare him off. He could also find out if all was as Kidd maintained. He listened to James Emott, appearing somewhat satisfied, but pointed out that any real documentary proof was lacking. In Emott's view, however, the governor gave the appearance of thinking that Kidd could request a pardon from the king and be reasonably sure of receiving it.

Meanwhile Kidd was sailing back and forth near Gardiner's Island, waiting. Finally Emott returned and brought with him Duncan Campbell, another friend of Kidd. They decided to return to Bellomont with two French documents that Kidd maintained he had found on ships captured in the Indian Ocean. Emott and Campbell also accompanied Governor Bellomont to the Massachusetts council to tell the council about talking with Kidd and give his side of the story.

The general opinion of the council was that Bellomont should negotiate with Kidd, and if his story appeared true—that he had been forced into piracy by his crew—then a pardon could be requested from the king. In essence Kidd's very life rested upon whether Bellomont was convinced that his story was true. Of course, having Kidd out of the picture would undoubtedly mean more of the treasure for the governor.

Bellomont sent the captain a friendly, reassuring letter, and believing in the governor's sincerity, Kidd set sail in the San Antonio to Boston, accompanied by Sarah. They stayed in Boston with their friend Duncan Campbell, and Captain Kidd and his wife shopped and were entertained. The captain was sometimes seen frequenting one of his favorite taverns, the Blue Anchor.

During the steamy days of the first week of July 1699 Kidd went before Bellomont and the council to defend himself. Asked for an accounting of his cargo, he gave it to them, and the council was astonished at the vast amount of goods. There were tons of sugar, saltpeter and iron, bales of fabric, 50 cannon, 80 pounds of silver and a 40-pound bag of gold. The councilors then asked for a specific written account of the voyage.

Kidd was unable to complete the narrative of his voyage of almost three years in the brief time he was given. He brought five of his men with him before the council, and they turned in sworn affidavits of their voyage.

The captain was also accompanied by his two friends—Campbell and Livingston. Bellomont held a 10,000-pound bond Livingston had put up for Kidd's appearances and cooperation. Undoubtedly the bond money was a temptation to Bellomont to keep because of his impecunious financial condition.

Forty-eight hours later the council sent for Captain Kidd again. When he appeared and told them he needed several days more to finish his written narrative of the voyage, they impatiently ordered him to bring it by five that afternoon. Bellomont signaled him in a friendly fashion as he rose to leave.

"When you return, come directly to my lodgings," he said, and Kidd nodded with some relief. Because the captain had always believed that he and Bellomont understood each other, he was sure that Bellomont's request must certainly mean his attitude was more friendly, and he was ready to help him.

Kidd returned to the small, sparsely furnished room at the inn near the waterfront and sat down at the oak table, where his quill pen scratched away laboriously. Several hours had passed when he heard the sound of pots and pans clattering in the kitchen below and knew it was the start of preparations for the evening meal. It was time for him to leave. He washed the ink stains off his fingers, thrust his arms through the sleeves of his well-tailored black coat and carefully arranged his perouke.

Hurriedly the captain turned the large key in the door to his room. Bellomont would be expecting him.

At a few minutes before five o'clock the captain, with a bundle of papers under his arm, walked briskly with the gait of a seafaring man along the ballast walkway that led to Bellomont's lodgings. He whistled a sea chantey as he went.

Suddenly Kidd felt himself seized from behind, but somehow he managed to wrench free. Evading the hands that clutched at him, he threw open the door of Bellomont's quarters and rushed inside.

"Bellomont! Bellomont!" he shouted. The governor stood there grimfaced. He made no answer.

At Kidd's heels appeared a constable and deputy. To his surprise Bellomont did not come to his aid but only looked on coldly while the constable secured his wrists with rope. They dragged him off to jail.

Kidd saw now that Bellomont had sprung a trap. The most profitable course for the impoverished governor had always been to arrest Kidd and confiscate the treasure. It would mean that much more profit for Bellomont after paying back the money he had borrowed to purchase his share of the enterprise. There would be a substantial treasure left for the governor.

The captain realized bitterly that he had become a political embarrassment. His wealthy former patrons had no desire to be associated with him or any enterprise that could be called piracy. They wished to see him speedily tried, but because of politics this did not take place. Captain William Kidd was taken from Boston to London in March of 1700 and imprisoned at Newgate. Here in this ghastly hellhole Kidd was held for a year, and his health deteriorated. Everything waited for the meeting of the newly elected parliament in the spring of 1701. The victors were supporters of the Old East India Company, Kidd's sworn enemy, and Tories, ready to punish the Whig-controlled junto. Now, events moved with a vengeance. When the trial took place Kidd was not provided with legal counsel and had to conduct his own defense. (Lawyers for the defense were allowed but could speak only to matters of law, not of fact.) Crucial evidence that might have proved embarrassing to his patrons was "misplaced."

The trial was brief, taking only two days, and Kidd was convicted first of the murder of the gunner, Moore, and then of piracy. Sentenced to die, Captain Kidd was hanged less than two weeks later on May 23, 1701.

"Bird food" some grimly called the blackened bodies dangling from wooden crosstrees decorating the banks of the Thames River. The display of rotting corpses moving grotesquely with the tide could be seen by both sailors and passers-by. Among them was the body of a man so legendary that his name had come to represent all that was believed heroic in buccaneering—Captain Kidd.

Anne Bonny
Carolina to West Indies

"It's hard to believe that you're really descended from a pirate!" Oliver Ravenel said to his friend. "Come sit down, and tell me more about the beautiful and infamous Anne Bonny." He led him over to a table at a bar on Charleston's Bay Street.

"Then let's order a round of rum." suggested John Fenwick.

"Was she really your ancestor?"

"None other." Fenwick reddened slightly.

"Did she ever reform?"

"I doubt if she ever became your typical Charleston lady, Oliver. But our story begins long before, when she was a young girl living with her father, William Cormac, at their plantation on the Black River. Let me share her story with you the way my great-grandmother often told it to me."

One summer afternoon in 1716 Anne appeared at the stable and asked the old groom, Romulus, to saddle Satan—a huge, black stallion.

"The master say you're not to ride him." The black man spoke kindly. "He say that horse too wild."

"You heard me!" Anne snapped, and she tossed her red head impatiently.

"Mistress Cormac, he done forbid me to saddle Satan for you. You know that." He tried to change the subject. "Why you put your hair up under your cap like that, Missy Cormac?" He was reproachful. "Cain't hardly tell you're a girl."

Her eyes glared at the dark, wizened face defiantly. "I said saddle him, Romulus!"

"Missy—your daddy'll have my hide."

"You dare disobey me?"

Her riding whip cracked, and Romulus leaped back so quickly that he fell over a wooden bucket and went sprawling to the ground. In seconds the slim figure dressed in boy's clothes entered the stall and expertly eased a bridle over the horse's head. She led the enormous black stallion out into the sunlight and swung lithely astride.

The old black man struggled to rise, as if to stop her, and Anne cracked her whip beside him as a warning. The noise spooked the barely broken stallion, and he reared back, his front feet pawing the air. Romulus stared up at the enormous animal with unspeakable terror seconds before the horse's feet came down on his face and his chest.

Horrified, Anne gazed down at the man's crushed, blood-covered features. Then she galloped off without finding out whether Romulus was dead or calling for help. By the time she returned one of the servants who had seen the old groom try to stop her had already told the girl's father. Romulus was dead, and Cormac was in a rage.

"Why didn't you stop and have someone take care of the man after Satan trampled him?" he demanded.

"I thought his chest had probably been crushed and nothing could be done," Anne replied coolly. "I was in a hurry."

"My God! You didn't even dismount. You left him without knowing whether he was dead or alive!" her father exploded. "Where were you going?"

"To meet my future husband."

"Husband!" he roared. "And who might that be?"

"James Bonny—a sailor."

"A sailor, be damned! Only when I am as dead as Romulus will you marry him! You can do better than that with your looks and my land."

"I'll choose whom I please," the girl replied, her green eyes flashing.

"The hell you will!" It was all he could do to keep from slapping her, and his big hands with the red-gold hair on the backs of them began to tremble. "A sailor! All he wants is your money."

Anne flew at him in a rage, her fists striking his face and chest, and he caught the flailing arms to hold her from him. He had that pinkish skin some redheads have which made him look even more flushed, and his breath came fast.

"You go to your room, young lady. We'll talk about this when you come down for dinner." She threw him a defiant glance and started up the curved staircase in the center of the elegant entrance hall. William Cormac watched her slim figure mount the stairs haughtily with almost catlike grace. Self-willed she was, but he still felt certain he could prevail upon her not to throw away her life by such a marriage.

"William Cormac was an Irish immigrant," Fenwick explained. "He was a prominent lawyer in Charles Towne as well as the owner of several plantations. He had tried to stay in Ireland with his lawfully wedded wife and had resolved what he regarded as a certain moral obligation by taking an 'unknown' little girl into his home. But someone had gossiped to Mrs. Cormac, and the suggestion that Anne was her husband's illegitimate child had so enraged his wife that she had threatened to send the girl away penniless. Cormac's response was to take Anne and his former mistress to America to begin a new life. Choosing the Charles Towne area, they were for awhile very happy, but Anne's mother succumbed to typhoid fever."

John continued, "In the years that followed, Cormac and his daughter were inseparable. She accompanied him everywhere he went, learning how to plant indigo, how to harvest rice, and most of the details of running his plantations. He could safely leave her in charge for a few days if he had to be away. But he knew now he had failed to impress upon her the role she must be ready to assume in Charles Towne society. She had become a young hoyden—not a young lady. Her language alone would crimp the hair of Charles Towne matrons, and even their daughters Anne's age would probably reach for their smelling salts. But what spirit the girl had!"

Two hours after their row, Cormac seated himself at the gleaming mahogany dining table to wait for his daughter. He sipped his Irish whiskey and waited. He poured a bit more, then withdrew his ornate gold pocket watch. His daughter was almost a quarter of an hour late for dinner. Cormac gulped the rest of the amber liquid down angrily, ready to storm upstairs after her—something he had never done.

He had just pushed back his mahogany chair when he heard the click of tiny heels at the top of the stairs. With maddening deliberation, Anne descended the stairs in a lime-colored dress that perfectly complemented her red hair. She appeared every inch a lady—which didn't deceive her father a bit. They ate in silence except for exchanging an occasional request to pass the silver platters of candied sweet potatoes, rice, fricasseed chicken, sliced ham, or beaten biscuits. Bacu, the Gullah maid, removed the fine china plates Cormac had brought with them from Ireland and set before them a dish of lemon trifle topped with a mound of whipped cream.

After they had finished, Anne sauntered over to the arch between the dining room and entrance hall and, looking up the stairs, announced, "Father, I believe I should like to have the wedding right here at home. I will come down these steps on your arm, and James and I can take our vows before the marble fireplace."

"You and James!" William Cormac spluttered over his third drink of whiskey, spraying a shower of tiny amber drops on the dark, glossy finish of the table. "No!" he exploded, striking the table with his fist until every piece of china rattled, and his tall-stemmed water goblet toppled over and rolled off, shattering into tiny shards of glittering crystal on the pine boards of the dark-polished floor.

"You'll choose no penniless sailor, by heaven," her father thundered. "If you marry that sea-going rascal, you won't inherit one clod of dirt from me!" And the stubborn Irishman meant exactly what he said. But he could not imagine what a tragic chain of events would result from this harshness toward a daughter as stubborn as himself.

That night Anne Cormac slipped out of the house, taking only enough of her possessions to fill a knapsack. She saddled Satan by the light of a small lantern and galloped off for Charles Towne. The next morning she posted a blunt note to her father: "Pick up Satan at the stable you use on Bay Street. Goodbye. —Anne."

She and James Bonny were married that same day, and Bonny, a ne'er-do-well seaman who had earned little respect among his fellow pirates, decided they would sail for the Bahamas. He had heard the governor was giving a reward to people who turned in pirates, and he immediately thought of selling the knowledge he had acquired on the Boston waterfront about the Brethren of the Sea. Anne quickly discovered that she had married a petty, jealous man, and when she found out that his livelihood came from turning in men who had once been his comrades, she had nothing but contempt for James Bonny.

It was only a matter of time until another man captured her eye, and that man was Jack Rackham, a dashing pirate captain. The two were immediately attracted to each other. Anne asked her husband for a divorce, which he refused.

"She doesn't love you, Bonny. I'll pay you a generous price for her, if you'll give her the divorce," Rackham said. Almost any man who was offered money for his wife would have challenged his rival to a duel, but not Bonny. He lacked the courage, and he felt a helpless fury.

"The answer is, no! And I'll tell the governor about her and have her beaten."

According to the law of the day the punishment for a woman who left her husband for another man was a public flogging. Though this punishment was seldom carried out, the governor threatened Anne with this treatment if she didn't return immediately to James Bonny. By this time Rackham was already plotting with Anne to steal a sloop and put to sea. When the governor's threat reached the pair, they accelerated their plans, and by dawn the next morning Rackham was sailing his new, ill-gotten ship with a new crew member on board—a woman.

Anne was faithful to her pirate captain. Writer Daniel Defoe says that a young crewman once made advances to Anne, and she beat him so badly that no one else tried to seduce her again. But she did give Rackham some jealous moments. After a time she became fast friends with a new pirate who had joined the crew, and the pair were constantly seen together, sometimes walking the deck arm-in-arm. This infuriated Captain Rackham.

"If I see you with that little fop again, I'll slit his throat!" he roared. In order to calm his rage, Anne asked that they have a private meeting with the new pirate in Rackham's cabin. He consented reluctantly, fingering the handle of his dagger and muttering, "I would rather solve the problem my way."

When the three were alone, Anne's pirate friend said in a soft voice, "I'm no threat to you, Captain Rackham." To Rackham's astonishment the pirate opened "his" shirt to partially reveal the breasts of a woman! The new crew member was a young widow named Mary Read, and she was the only woman friend Anne had ever known. Later Mary married one of the crewmen, and she and Anne remained close friends.

Then Anne began to have a much more serious problem. To her distress, she noticed her agility lessening, her footing becoming unsteady, and her dagger thrusts finding their mark less often as she fought the crews of the vessels Rackham plundered. Sometimes, to her humiliation, her blows missed altogether. She was pregnant.

When Anne told Rackham, he suggested that they put aside piracy briefly and seek a more peaceful environment. They sailed for Cuba—a haven for pirate families, where husbands returned periodically for whatever semblance of home life pirates could have. Some women stayed there the year around, but not Anne, for she loved the sea. Scarcely risen from her childbed, she gave the baby up to another family in the pirate colony and was soon back on board ship, fighting at Rackham's side, capturing and plundering one ship after another.

During October of 1720, Rackham's ship *Curlew* attracted the interest of the governor of Jamaica. He had given the Brethren of the Sea offers of pardon if they would surrender, and many had done so. But some of the more stubborn had lacked gratitude for this generous treatment, and Rackham was one of them. This angered the governor, who sent an armed British sloop to attack the pirate captain's vessel.

The sloop took the *Curlew* by surprise. Soldiers and marines clambered over the side with swords drawn and revolvers firing. After running two Britishers through with her sword, Anne Bonny turned just in time to catch sight of most of her fellow pirates scrambling down the ladder to take refuge below deck. Captain Rackham, too, disappeared, and she and Mary Read, with the help of one man, found themselves holding off the attackers.

"Come up and fight, you sea scum!" Anne called out. Mary angrily fired her pistols into the hold to shame—perhaps rally—the crew, killing one pirate and wounding several others. "Fight, you cowards, or you'll hang!" Anne raged at them from the top of the ladder, but neither Rackham nor any of his crew emerged from the hold to defend themselves.

"Surrender! We don't want to kill women," a British marine shouted to Anne and Mary.

Then one of the soldiers closed in and began tearing at the beautiful red-haired pirate's clothing. Whirling, Anne jabbed him in the groin with a blow of her knee. "Get back! I'll die before you bloody scoundrels touch me."

"Let her alone!" shouted an officer, and he grasped her with a vise-like grip. "You wildcat!" he said with some respect as she continued to fight him. "Be still, and I'll make sure that you're not molested."

At the same time Anne glanced up to see the ominous black pirate flag of the *Curlew* lowered and the British Union Jack being raised in its stead. She ceased struggling. Everyone aboard was taken prisoner, and the two women, so that they would not be subjected to crude remarks, were led to the captain's cabin.

When the pirates were tried in Jamaica, spectators jammed the courtroom of St. Jago de la Vega. Crewmen who were able to prove they had been forced into piracy were soon acquitted, and Mary Read's husband was one of them. But there could be no plea of "being forced" for Anne Bonny and Mary Read. Both were still defiant, and the testimony of the crew members of the *Curlew* did not help them.

"No one was more ready to attack a ship and fight in hand-to-hand combat than these two women," the men testified. Their accounts of the women's ferocity horrified spectators and jury alike.

Anne Bonny, pregnant for the second time, entered the courtroom, striking even in tattered men's clothing.

"Look at that red-haired monster," women murmured as she passed. "To think she's going to be a mother!" The male spectators and even officers of the court regarded her warily, as if she were a tigress who might leap at them. But many found it impossible not to admire the proud way she held herself, staring straight before her, head high, oblivious to insulting remarks. There was a hush as she passed through the crowd, for she drew their attention like a magnet.

"Anne's trial attracted considerable interest," Fenwick went on, "and some who came to hear it were South Carolinians engaged in trade between Charles Towne and Jamaica. Among those who listened to the prisoner's testimony was wealthy Robert Fenwick, owner of Fenwick Castle, a South Carolina barony near Charles Towne." He broke off and smiled at Ravenel. "Yes, my great-great grandfather." Motioning to the waitress for another glass of rum, he continued his story.

As the trial proceeded, Jack Rackham was sentenced to be hanged at Gallows Point, Port Royal. The punishment Anne would receive was obvious to her from the moment she heard the "guilty" verdict for Rackham and the other pirates. But the spectators sat in suspense waiting to hear Anne's sentence. Everyone knew Chief Justice Sir Nicholas Laws was a "hanging judge." Nor did he waver in this case.

His verdict was "guilty," and Anne was to "be hanged by the neck until dead."

Then, with her beautiful, sea-water green eyes gazing at the chief justice imploringly, Anne made her final plea. "May it please the court," she said in surprisingly soft, feminine tones, "it is my understanding that the courts of England and her colonies will not execute sentence of death on any woman while she is quick with child. Though I plead guilty to the charge of piracy, I ask for clemency by reason of being with child, and so does Mary Read."

The courtroom was thrown into an uproar. The condition of Mary Read was a surprise. After debate the spokesman announced that "the two women will be held until proper jury can inquire into the case, as the problem of pirates quick with child has never before come up." The judge delayed her execution.

Two weeks after her baby was born in prison, Anne was reprieved, and her hope for freedom seemed to have come true. Then, strangely and unexpectedly, she was re-sentenced. She had accepted the news of her coming death bravely when—without explanation—her sentence was remitted at the last minute. She was to be freed. But a few days later she was once again condemned to death. Finally, after so much bizarre behavior on the part of the judge, she was unexpectedly released for good! Gossip in Jamaica had it that considerable influence on the part of someone rich and powerful had been exerted on her behalf.

Less than 20 years old, Anne was as lovely as she had ever been, and she was free to start a new life. To the surprise of everyone—for the beautiful young woman pirate had by now become a public figure—she and her baby disappeared mysteriously within hours after her last release. Robert Fenwick was said to have spirited her back with him to Charles Towne, where she became mistress of Fenwick Castle.

They should have lived happily ever after. But according to a Charles Towne story, Fenwick found her bedroom empty late one night after a party, and two English thoroughbred horses missing from his stable. He suspected that Anne had run off with a lover, and, summoning the help of the servants, he pursued and caught the pair. Robert Fenwick himself slipped a noose around the man's neck and led the horse under a live oak, tying the rope over a branch. He forced Anne to lash the rump of her lover's horse with her whip, and with one frantic leap the horse dashed off and left the young man dangling.

Fenwick made Anne watch while her paramour grasped the rope with both hands, supporting the weight of his body for as long as he could until his arms began to tremble and his fingers finally slipped from the rope. She was forced to view his agony—his face grotesque in the moonlight and his tongue protruding horribly—until suddenly, the rope broke. Half-conscious, he fell to the ground with blood spurting from his ears and nose. When he revived and begged for his life, Fenwick ordered his servants to lift him again to the tree limb. The young man drew his knees to his chest and then straightened them convulsively, the veins swelling in his neck as if they would burst.

Anne Bonny cried great gasping sobs as she watched her lover's death throes. Then, as she turned to gallop angrily back to the house, she saw a servant riding up with a small figure. It was her daughter, still half asleep, and she held out her arms to take the child.

"Shall I wake her so that she can see her mother's lover?" Fenwick asked Anne.

"Oh, no! For God's sake, no!" Anne cried out. Perhaps she had lost some of her hardness in the years since arriving in Charles Towne.

"Then swear you will not betray me again."

"I swear that I will not."

"And that you will behave?"

"Yes."

"For if you don't, you will simply disappear, Anne. I shall take you to some isolated island and maroon you. Do you believe me?"

"I believe you," she said quietly, and she knew that he would do exactly as he threatened. Not at all intimidated by Anne, he had more in common with her than any spectator in that Jamaica courtroom, for, although few knew it, Robert Fenwick had been one of the Red Sea pirates. After years of plundering ships thousands of miles away, he had settled in Charles Towne and built a reputation as a respected, law-abiding citizen.

"And that's the story of the taming of my pirate ancestor, Anne Bonny," John Fenwick said, gazing out the window toward the bay.

"Great heavens! You are a descendant of two pirates," exclaimed Oliver, drawing back in mock horror. "No wonder I have sometimes thought you such a reckless sort, John."

"There are probably other pirate descendants like myself alive here in Charleston today. Maybe they've become ruthless acquisitions directors for some large corporation blowing other companies out of the water!" He pushed his glass from him, glanced down at his watch and ran strong, restless fingers through his auburn hair.

"Well, my boat leaves early tomorrow morning, and after so long on land, I'm ready to put to sea. It's probably where I'm happiest. Goodnight, friend."

And as the tall, broad-shouldered figure rose from the captain's chair, for an instant, Oliver Ravenel seemed to see the brilliant flash of light on the metal of a cutlass hanging at his friend's waist. Then the door of the dockside pub closed behind Fenwick, and he disappeared into the night.

John Redfield
American Coast to Red Sea

The return voyage to America from the West Indies had been an easy one, and now the *San Antonio* edged toward the shoreline of Carolina, north of the Cape of Fear. Two men stood at the prow, one listening respectfully while the other spoke in low tones.

"Redfield, I shall have to entrust you with an important service. I've been generous with the crew, as you know, but I'm still somewhat, shall we say, overstocked. I cannot possibly arrive in port at New York or Boston with such cargo as I am carrying. I am going to deposit some of my treasure here, and I'm going to make an unusual request of you. I want you to settle here near its location and watch over it for me for awhile. The climate is pleasant, and you'll receive a thousand pounds in gold for your own pocket, my friend."

"Your wishes are my orders, sir."

"Then, my friend, swear by the Holy Virgin that you will faithfully watch over the chests; that you will touch none of their contents, nor give information that could lead to their discovery."

"Nothing could make me betray your trust, sir."

"Also, do not disclose to any one why you have chosen this isolated place to make your home."

Captain John Redfield raised his right hand. "I give you my solemn pledge, sir."

Captain William Kidd pounded him on the shoulder in his hearty way, saying, "You're a man I have always trusted, Captain John. I remember that day years ago when your warning saved me from a knife thrust in battle." He had continued to call his friend "captain" although Redfield no longer had a ship of his own to command.

"Put to shore," Redfield ordered the pilot.

"Of course, there are conditions," Kidd went on. "Keep this agreement for five years. If by then I haven't returned, you are free to dig up the smaller chest and use half of its contents, leaving the other half, which I may still return and demand. The same conditions apply to the larger chest for a second period of five years."

After each condition Redfield gravely nodded assent. His loyalty to Kidd was obvious.

"But when the time comes that I have need of the treasure I will send you an order for part of it," continued Kidd, at the same time pressing something small and hard into Redfield's palm. "Look for the imprint of this signet to prove that my written order is genuine."

Redfield opened his hand and stared down at the small piece of resin lying in his palm. Upon it were stamped Captain Kidd's intertwined initials.

"I will not surrender a single coin without this, sir," Redfield promised.

The moon would be up soon, and Kidd called two of his most trusted seamen. He and the captain proceeded to the ship's lockers that opened into his cabin, laboriously dragged out two iron chests and had the men carry them to the outer deck. They secured the chests well with ropes and lowered them into the boats, along with shovels, axes and firearms. The rowers took their positions, and Kidd and Redfield climbed down the rope ladder into the stern.

"Ply the oars," ordered Redfield softly. No one spoke as the small boats glided away from the *San Antonio*, which soon became a large, black shape receding behind them. Nearing the Carolina coast that night in May of 1699, Kidd and Redfield's boat entered an inlet, following one winding passage after another among the cypress trees of the marsh until finally the bow scraped sand at the edge of the island. The seamen dragged their small craft well up beyond the tide and the two captains walked into the dense trees and undergrowth, soon disappearing from view. Captain Kidd wanted the location to be secluded but a place they could measure off with permanent landmarks. The two men stood in the moonlight, patiently waiting while Kidd and Redfield searched. After awhile the men heard voices, and saw the captains reappear on the beach.

Led by a circuitous route, the seamen accompanied Kidd and Redfield to the hiding place they had chosen. Pointing out two marked trees about ten feet apart, Kidd directed the pair to dig. Nothing could be heard for a while but the sound of their increasingly heavy breathing as they dug deeper and deeper. Then they lowered the chests down into sandy pits, marking each by a cross of branches. Last, and very carefully in order not to damage the roots, they planted two small trees, one beside each hole.

The tiny island now held enough wealth to buy several English castles.

The next night Captain Redfield made a trip ashore alone, hiding the money Kidd had given him for his own use at three places. He would need it when he returned.

The *San Antonio* then set sail on a northward course and did not stop until the pirates reached Albemarle Sound for their rendezvous with other buccaneers. Captains Kidd and Redfield sauntered along the deck, enjoying the warm spring sunshine. They had recently made a successful voyage among the Spanish colonies to the south, and Kidd was lavishly dressed after the manner of a Spanish cavalier. He wore a cocked hat with a yellow band boasting a black plume, a knee length coat of black velvet, blue trousers with gold buckles and large silver buckles on his shoes. The Carolina authorities would have given much to see him—and more to capture the notorious Kidd!

Here the pirates feasted for several days, and while the crew entertained themselves, Kidd fitted Captain Redfield with a small sloop and provisions. So that the rest of the crew might not ask questions, Redfield left one morning before sunrise for his new home on the Carolina coast. Kidd had selected four strong men to accompany his friend to build living quarters—men who thought they would like colonizing, and who, of course, knew nothing of the treasure buried nearby. With genuine reluctance he bade them and Redfield goodbye. William Kidd felt an unaccustomed foreboding. He had no idea whether it was for himself or Redfield.

With benefit of good weather, a comfortable house had been built. Redfield and the men then set about hewing out a clearing for a more permanent settlement. Hunting and fishing were ample relaxation after their labors, for the land was rich in game, and they passed the days contentedly enough. When they grew restless they boarded the sloop, exploring other new settlements to the north, and to the south—Charles Towne was growing quickly.

Redfield named his new home Rindout, and in the summer of the second year, he found a wife—a jolly, quick-witted Irish girl from near Charles Towne who settled in quite happily. More than a year and a half passed without incident. No visitors arrived at their settlement, not even a solitary Indian brave. But one October morning Captain Redfield sighted a ship lying off the inlet. The sight caused quite a stir among the men, and Redfield wondered whether the ship belonged to Captain Kidd. Should he go out to the vessel himself? His natural caution asserted itself, however, and despite the excitement he decided to wait for the ship to show its intentions.

After several hours, Redfield could see a boat approaching shore, and he and his men recognized the flag at its prow as the ensign of Captain Kidd. They hastily began preparations to welcome him, but as the boat drew near, the impressive figure of Kidd was not visible. In the captain's place instead sat Max Brisbau, a former crew member who Redfield remembered had also served under Kidd. He was not displeased to see him, but he couldn't help wondering at

Kidd's choice of an emissary. Brisbau had not been a favorite among the crew or with Kidd.

The man alighted, greeting him effusively, and when John Redfield began to ask questions Brisbau put up his hand with a smile to interrupt him, smoothly explaining that he had come in the service of the captain and would later communicate the object of his visit. In the time since Rindout was built, Redfield had often been lonely, and in his pleasure now at seeing any of his former shipmates, he was hospitable. A half dozen of Brisbau's crew came ashore, too, and all were received with enthusiasm by Redfield's men, who were eager as he to hear news of the outside world.

In the afternoon Brisbau, over a glass of ale, divulged the reason for his visit. "I have an order from Captain Kidd to remove two chests of treasure hidden in the neighborhood. You are to be awarded a generous amount, and your guardianship of the treasure will cease."

Redfield started to speak, but Brisbau went on. "I want to convey the gracious thanks of our captain for your faithfulness. Kidd instructed me to send you his highest esteem. His words were, 'I know of no man in whom I have more confidence than Captain John Redfield.'"

This was flattering to hear, but Redfield still hesitated. He nodded his thanks, but his reply was guarded.

"It may or may not be true that Captain Kidd has buried possessions in this immediate locality. Undoubtedly he has secreted treasure along this coast, but the question is where? I have *some* knowledge of possible hiding places, but I must have a written order over the captain's signature and his personal seal before I can disclose it."

"Of course." Brisbau reached for his inner coat pocket to remove the document but, failing to find it, he cursed with a show of great annoyance.

"Blast me! It must be on the table of my cabin back at my ship. I'll send someone back immediately to get it."

Then he shook his head dismissively as if on second thought.

"How ridiculous! Just come over to our vessel. We'll have a drink of rum, and I can give you the paper over there."

Captain Redfield pleaded other duties, and Brisbau became angry. "You're insulting me by your blasted stubbornness," he shouted.

Redfield was now convinced that Brisbau was engaged in treachery. "I'll give you no information until you hand over a proper written order with the captain's seal," said he.

Leaping up, Brisbau shouted, "I'll have that treasure or your life will be worth no more than Jack Kettle's, who flaunted his opposition before Captain Kidd himself."

He had hardly spoken when Captain Redfield, aware that the other man was armed and he was not, saw that his only hope was to spring first at Brisbau. Brisbau moved slightly to one side. He wore a sword, and from his belt hung also a pistol and a wicked-looking knife. The advantage must be gained swiftly. Redfield had missed the hold he had tried for—to secure both arms—but he grasped Brisbau's right arm tightly with his left hand and held the man's wrist in his right, his grip strong as a vise.

But he could not disarm him. Redfield knew that when he tired Brisbau would be able to wrest himself from his grip and then dispatch him with his knife or pistol. He must not give Brisbau the opportunity to use those weapons.

Thinking himself alone in the house, he had not cried out. However, just as he felt he could not maintain his grip much longer, he heard a sound in the hall. Mrs. Redfield entered the room.

"My God, John," she exclaimed, and to his despair, she ran from the room. But she had quickly assessed the situation. A moment later she was back with a rope, which she looped around Brisbau's shoulders, tightened, and wound about his arms until he was powerless to resist. Redfield now tied the enraged but helpless Brisbau to a chair.

He pondered what to do about his prisoner. His men had gone on an excursion along the coast for the entertainment of their guests, and when they seemed slow in returning, Redfield began to wonder whether the situation would come to a conflict between his men and

Brisbau's.

Until this hour he had confided nothing of Kidd's secret to his wife, but now he explained the matter fully. Mrs. Redfield thought that perhaps Brisbau's claim was just. "Couldn't you settle with him for part of the treasure?" she asked.

"He has presented no paper to me from Kidd. He has no claim to it. The treasure was to be kept for the captain. Besides, do you think Brisbau would accept part of the treasure and then leave?"

Mrs. Redfield considered this for a moment and then shook her head.

An hour passed, and one of Redfield's men returned. The captain immediately saw that his man was ill at ease. His eyes would not meet Redfield's. Finally he spoke.

"We have reached an agreement with Brisbau's men that all of us will share in the treasure," said he, "but we will do you no harm. We will discuss it when all the men have returned."

The captain was so angry he thought of attacking the fellow and punishing him for his treachery, but he restrained himself, knowing that the odds were overwhelmingly against this tactic succeeding since his own men were joining Brisbau. Fuming, he waited for the men to return. They released Brisbau, then began to question Redfield about the location of the treasure.

Redfield pleaded with his men to stand by him. None would do so. On learning of the hidden riches they had eagerly become confederates of Brisbau's.

"We'll give you a full share, if you show us its location," one of Redfield's men tried to persuade him.

"And if you don't, you and your wife will be treated like prisoners," cut in Brisbau furiously.

But Redfield's men gave Brisbau to understand that they were in charge of the situation and that he must curb his anger toward Redfield. All of them had to work together to extract information, and angering the captain further would not help.

"You have no credentials, and I've given my pledge," Redfield replied firmly.

Sure they could find the treasure unaided, the men scoured the woods, growing angrier as the fruitless search dragged on. Brisbau ordered the captain and his wife put in chains. The men alternately urged and threatened, but Redfield could not be made to give them the slightest information. Only the protective intervention of Redfield's men kept Brisbau from torturing the captain.

Suddenly Brisbau had another idea. Loading Redfield and his wife on board his ship, he set off on a short cruise, planning to threaten Redfield with what would appear an accidental death at sea. But before he could carry out this plan, the men, wearied with the long struggle, decided they would put in at Charles Towne for rum and entertainment.

The ship was in the harbor when she was hailed by port authorities and stopped for papers. Brisbau could not produce anything to prove that his was a legitimate cargo ship, so he was immediately suspected of piracy and seized with all the men. When the ship was searched, Redfield and his wife were discovered, chained as prisoners, and released. He told the authorities that he was a property owner north of Charles Towne who had been kidnapped by a pirate and his crew, and they let him go free.

Based on Redfield and his wife's testimony, Brisbau and his men were imprisoned and barely escaped the hangman's noose.

After he heard of Kidd's execution for piracy in England, Redfield left the isolated area where he had built his home, and he and his wife settled in Charles Towne—as many another pirate would do through the years. Here he became an industrious, respected citizen, and any suspicion of a connection with buccaneers was soon forgotten. Always considered a wealthy man, Redfield was known to be hard working, and all believed his land holdings and successful business ventures had come about through wise investments and his own enterprise—not through judicious withdrawals of cached pirate treasure!

The secret of the family's wealth was kept closely guarded for generations. Only years later did Redfield's son divulge it to his own grandson, who put it in writing nearly a century and a half after the precious booty of Captain Kidd was hidden. The name of the little booklet was "Money Island."

Edward Low
New England to South Atlantic

"Lemme alone! Quit it or I'll tell our old man," the little boy bawled at the top of his lungs.

"Oh, no yer won't!" A larger boy was sitting on the smaller one's chest, pummeling his already bloody face. "If you do, I'll tell him what you did to get that money. Give it to me!"

"Won't do it!"

"Sold that bottle of his, ya did. Found where he had it hid."

"I didn't neither!" screamed the child. The heavy-set, straw-haired boy on top of him grabbed his arm and began to twist it.

"Ow-w-ch!" he shrieked. " 'At's my broken arm."

"I know it. Give big brother the money."

He gave the arm a particularly vicious turn.

"Quit! I'll give it ya."

"All of it?"

The little boy with the dirty, tear-streaked face shrieked, "All of it, Eddie."

"Stop blubberin', crybaby. Turn your pockets out."

The money tumbled on the ground, and the pudgy-faced twelve-year-old boy had it in a lightning flash. Disappearing among the people along the crowded street of Westminster, England, he sauntered along with a pretense of casualness until he saw a redheaded girl approaching him. She saw him, too, and dodged into the entrance of a craftsman's shop, but he was too quick for her. With the rapidity of a striking snake he grasped the back of her dress and held her fast.

"Me sister," he explained to the startled man who stood up from his workbench to see what was happening.

"I'm not his sister!"

"Brat," Eddie yelled at her. "Shut up," and he shoved her out into the street, where he put his mouth up to her ear.

"Listen fast, Ellie," he muttered. "This afternoon when yer ma gives ya money to go to the store, I'll be waitin' and ya better give me half of it."

"But if I don't come back with everything—the beef and potatoes and turnips and flour—she'll beat me!" the girl whined.

"Tell her ya lost part of the money."

"But . . ."

"But nothin'!" he interrupted, slapping her across the mouth. "Remember what happened the time you didn't give me the money?" His hand moved over her thin buttocks, and he leered at her with eyes unexpectedly cruel for one so young. "I'll be waitin' for ya. Better have it, Ellie." She began to weep softly but gulped assent.

There were bushes and a few scrubby trees in back of the small shack the Low family rented, and this was where Eddie now headed. His younger brother would be too frightened to come home tonight. Ronald, the brother two years older than he, worked as an apprentice craftsman for one of the shopkeepers. Eddie sat casually at the edge of the privet bushes until he was sure no one was around, then disappeared among them to hide the money in his secret place. Emerging cautiously a little later, he strolled up to the house, whistling a sea chantey. He could hear the sound of his ma crying, but that wasn't unusual. Evidently the old man had waked up and was at her about something. Sure enough, as Eddie reached the house he heard a hoarse voice shouting, "Where's my rum, you old hag?"

No wonder his father's nickname was "Rummy." When Eddie stepped into the doorway, he saw that his mother had a bruise from her cheekbone across to her chin, and he felt an unaccustomed pang.

"Tell me where ya hid it, woman!" Barney Low was shouting. Eddie's mother saw her son enter, and his father caught the sudden softening of her expression. Low's swollen, bleary-eyed face turned toward his son.

"You're the one what took it," he accused, striding toward Eddie and seizing his shoulder with a huge, dirty paw. "Gi' me that money." He raised an arm to strike the boy. Eddie's mother tried to deflect the blow, but the drunken Barney shoved her roughly out of his way.

"Don' know what you're talkin' about," protested Eddie. He could smell his sour breath, he was so close.

The big man's left fist shot forward against the boy's face, delivering a blow that sent him flying in the direction of the fireplace.

"I think ya do!" And he came lumbering toward his son.

Eddie picked up the poker and raised it.

"Hit yer own father, would ya?" Barney bellowed.

"Lemme alone! I'll . . ." Eddie's voice, filled with panic, trailed off. If he gave the money back he was a goner, and if he didn't . . . it would be all the same.

The big man lunged, and at that instant Eddie swung. Low dived into the blow, increasing its force, and Eddie heard the poker, like the sound of a mule's kick, strike the side of his father's head. Rummy Low dropped to the floor. Mother and son stood for several seconds, staring at him as he lay there, the side of his head bashed in above the ear, blood spurting from it. He didn't move.

Eddie knelt down and opened the tattered, dirty shirt. He put his ear against the massive chest.

"He's dead, mum."

They talked about what to do next and decided that Eddie would stay with the body while his mother went to his older brother's place for help. Eddie sat and looked at the crumpled figure on the floor, smelling the scent of rum in the closeness of the fetid little room.

Drunk. Always drunk, he thought with disgust.

Eddie sighed and pulled a little game from his pocket—small sticks of wood, which he arranged and rearranged to pass the time. He was asleep when, in the early morning hours, his brother pulled up with his old wagon and mule.

Ronald Low glanced briefly at his father's body. "Sorry, mum. But if it had 'a happened sooner, 'twould have been better for us all." He had a sunburned face with high cheekbones and a wide, kind mouth. A tall, strong fellow—better built than Eddie.

Hoisting Rummy Low's heavy, inert form into the back of the wagon, Ron and Eddie covered it with sacks and climbed up on the wagon seat. When the mule reached a heavily wooded area, Ron jerked on the reins for the animal to stop. They found the place where the brush was thickest and the ground the softest, and when they had dug a hole deep enough, they rolled their sack-wrapped burden into it.

All day they hid near Ron's, thinking the police might come to question them about their father's disappearance, but no one at Rummy's usual haunts cared when he didn't show up. In the gathering shadows of dusk they walked quickly along the waterfront, soon hiring on a merchant vessel due to leave at sunup.

Both were quick to learn seamanship and both were hard workers, but they were never chummy. Ron was quiet. He liked to whittle. He hummed sea chanteys as he scrubbed the deck or adjusted the rigging. He rarely drank, while Eddie rarely stopped drinking. Boastful and pushy around the crewmen, the boy Eddie had an air of recklessness. The one person he sometimes talked about with love—seemed almost to worship—was his mother back in England.

The merchant ship finally put in for several weeks at Boston, and, tired of life at sea, Eddie decided to make Boston his home. He began work at a ship rigging house, and the master of the company praised him for his good work. His ship left for Barbados, Ron shipping out with it.

Several years passed, and Eddie, worried about his mother, decided to pay a visit home to England.

"Well. Ain't you the one for surprises," said his mother with a snaggle-toothed smile. His father had knocked out some of her teeth. "You've grown into quite the man." His shoulders were broad and muscular from handling the heavy rigging.

Eddie stayed on in Westminster for a few weeks until he got restless—his mother had married some bloke he didn't like. Telling her goodbye, he sailed back to Boston and his work at the rigging house. But gradually his discontent grew, and his explosive temper, always lurking just beneath the surface, boiled over. There was an ugly quarrel over the way he said some rigging should be done, and he pitched a heavy coil of rope at his master, who was caught off balance and fell. The master's left arm was limp when he rose, but he managed to strike out with his right, using an end of rope that grazed Eddie's face as he dodged out the door.

Making the rounds of one pub after another along the waterfront, whom should Eddie meet but Ron. His ship was in port.

"You done it again, I see," said Ron.

"Whatcha talkin' about?"

"Been fightin'. Get yourself fired?"

"Maybe—I hate these damn New Englanders!"

"Why?"

"Blasted superior know-it-alls. I'll make 'em sorry someday."

Ron shook his head and grunted in disgust. But he got Eddie hired on his sloop leaving Boston at dawn. It was bound for the Bay of Honduras, and Eddie boarded it that night, sleeping by his brother's side on deck, for it was unseasonably warm and humid. The ship was delayed by several early fall storms, and when they finally got to Honduras they found the bay a busy tropical port filled with cargo ships carrying fruit, "barrills of rum," "hoggsheads" of beef, pork, and sugar and European goods.

Eddie's brash confidence and boasts about his seamanship soon attracted the attention of another ship's captain, who put him in command of a boat employed to bring logs of wood to his vessel.

Wood was so badly needed that Eddie Low was given 12 armed men to seize it by force from Spaniards along the coast. Despite his misgivings about the work, Ron decided to go with his brother; the money, compared to an ordinary seaman's pay, was hard to resist.

For a week all went well. Then the captain made a remark that angered Eddie. Enraged, he drew his pistol and shot at the captain, but the bullet hit another man instead. The brothers and armed crew escaped in the boat. The next day Eddie Low hoisted a black flag, seized a small vessel and embarked on a career of piracy.

They soon captured another ship, and Low made a Charles Harris captain of the smaller. Sailing the *Fancy*, Low mounted ten guns on her and manned her with a crew of 50 men. As they pursued two ships that were sailing southward from Boston, a terrible hurricane overtook them, and the crew labored both day and night to save their lives, throwing six heavy guns overboard to lighten their vessel. Next went most of their provisions. During the storm Low's and Harris's ships became separated. When the weather improved, their prey—the two ships from Boston—was gone, and there was no sign of Harris's ship. Captain Low had to go into a small island harbor west of the Caribees to refit his vessels and exchange what cargo they had left for provisions.

On his way to the Azores, Low discovered a better weapon than guns, the one used so effectively by the Assyrian armies. That weapon was terror.

Captain Low had captured a French ship with 34 guns and was taking her with him as he entered St. Michael's roads, when he saw seven sailing vessels at anchor. He threatened any masters on the vessels who opposed him with instant death, and without firing a shot the seven ships surrendered. In need of supplies, Low sent a demand to the governor for water and fresh provisions as his condition for releasing the vessels; otherwise, he said, he would put them to the torch.

The governor immediately complied, and from the shore he and other local officials watched through their glasses and waited. Six of the ships set sail, but the seventh, a French vessel, did not. Low had seized her guns and all her men, except for the cook.

"He's a greasy fellow and should fry well!" he said, lifting a bottle of rum to his lips. Over his brother Ron's furious protests, Edward Low had the terrified man bound to the mast and then gave orders to set the vessel afire. Even Low's hardened crew were aghast, but they did not dare show it.

Their next prey was the *Wright Galley*, commanded by a Captain Carter, who tried to defend his ship. Low's crew cut and mangled him in a barbarous manner. When they found two Portuguese priests on board, they seized and bound them, then lowered them several times into the sea until they drowned. Ron was at least a nominal Catholic, and this didn't set well with him, nor with a horrified Portuguese seaman who stood by his side watching. Unfortunately the Portuguese man was observed by a member of Low's crew.

"I don't like the look on your stupid face!" he shouted and slashed the man across the body with his cutlass, instantly killing him. This action started a slaughter. Some were for burning the galley as they had the French vessel, but instead they began to slash the rigging and sails to pieces. Low then set the remainder of the *Wright*'s crew adrift on their ravaged vessel, at the mercy of the sea.

Thoroughly disgusted with his brother, Ron was now determined to leave the *Fancy*, and when they made port a few days later he hired on with another vessel.

Edward Low and his crew sailed on to the Canary Islands, and there, one of his two ships was overturned on the careen and sunk as the hull was being cleaned. Now only the *Fancy* remained. A hundred pirates boarded her and set sail to find new spoils. The first ship crossing their path was a Portuguese vessel that sturdily resisted them. When the infuriated Captain Low captured her, he began to torture the men to learn where they kept the ship's monies.

"The money bag was hung out the window!" one man finally revealed.

"Where?"

"The cabin . . . cabin," cried the fellow, but when they reached it all they found was the end of the rope from which the money had been suspended. During the chase the captain had cut the rope and allowed the bag of 11,000 gold coins to fall into the sea.

Edward Low exploded into a rage, storming and cursing the captain.

"Cut off his lying lips!" he ordered one of the pirates. "Broil them before his eyes!" Now, in a murderous orgy, the pirates fell upon the Portuguese captain and his crew and murdered them all, then set the ship adrift after cutting her sails and rigging to pieces.

After cleaning the *Fancy* on an island, they set out for the Bay of Honduras, and as they prepared to enter the bay, they met a Spanish vessel coming out. Low deceptively hoisted the Spanish flag, and the ship allowed them to come alongside. As the *Fancy* came near, Captain Low quickly hoisted the black flag, and the *Spaniard* was seized with no resistance. To the astonishment of Low and his pirates, they found five English masters held prisoner aboard from ships the Spaniards had captured along with English goods. The English ships accompanied them in a flotilla the *Spaniard* was leading.

Low gave the command to murder all the Spaniards, and in a frenzy he and his crew set upon them with every sort of weapon imaginable.

"Send out a canoe!" he shouted when he saw some of the Spaniards trying to escape his merciless hands by leaping into the sea. A canoe was sent out to murder those trying to swim ashore. This done, Low plundered the Spanish vessel and then restored the English masters to their respective ships, for reasons only Edward Low himself could have known. Then he set the *Spaniard* afire.

After the *Spaniard*, Low went on to capture 19 ships in succession between the Leeward Islands and the mainland, treating their crews—especially those from New England—with a barbarity unusual even among pirates. His pirating career had continued now for almost a decade, and he was feared from Boston down the length of the Atlantic coast and southward throughout the East Indies. Sometimes his actions shocked even his own crew, a fact which was finally to end the career of this seafaring, pillaging villain.

As Low cruised between the Leeward Islands and the mainland, seeking victims, whom should he meet but Harris, whose ship had been separated from Low's during the terrible storm. It happened that a sleek vessel called the *Greyhound* was sailing along the coast, too. When the commander of that ship, with its 20 guns and crew of 120 men, heard that the pirate Edward Low was not far away, he went out to search for him. The *Greyhound* soon sailed into view of the *Fancy*, commanded by Low himself, and the *Ranger*, commanded by Harris. The pirates saw it as a particularly fine ship and set out to follow the *Greyhound*, sailing just behind it.

To their surprise, she swiftly turned about and faced them. The *Fancy* and the *Ranger* hurriedly hoisted black flags, each firing a gun.

Coming within musket shot, the *Greyhound* hauled up her mainsail, clapped close upon a wind to keep the pirates from running to leeward and engaged them. Low and Harris, realizing for the first time that they were dealing with a British man-of-war, edged away under her stern. Now, the tables were turned.

With the *Greyhound* pursuing them, the pirates made a running fight for about two hours, but there was little wind. Using their oars, the two pirate sloops were pulling considerably ahead of the *Greyhound*, so she stopped firing and all hands manned the oars. At three in the afternoon the man-of-war overtook Low and Harris, and the fight began again, each side firing steadily until the *Greyhound* blasted away the mainyard of the *Ranger*.

"Fight, you bloody devils, fight!" screamed Low's quartermaster on the *Fancy*. Beside him he could see that Charles Harris' men on the *Ranger* were attacking furiously. But Captain Low, the man who held such a reputation for boldness and was a terror to his own men, abandoned the *Ranger* to the enemy, and the *Fancy* fled.

In the opinion of some of those present, Low's conduct was both cowardly and amazing, for the man-of-war could probably not have hurt the two ships, if Low had commanded his men half as courageously as did Harris. Low's escape was a narrow one. It would seem that this scare might have been a warning to him and his crew, but it was not. Nothing could change the ways of these hardened men, and they renewed their violence and brutality on the next ship they captured, treating the captain with wanton cruelty and finally shooting him to death.

Low forced the crew of that ship into a small boat, giving them only a compass and a little water, and left them adrift 80 miles from land. Surprisingly, the men eventually reached shore.

Of all the English pirates, none was as barbarous as Edward Low. He took men's lives when he was in a good humor as readily as he did in the grip of anger. On one occasion when he captured a Virginian, Low shoved an enormous bowl of punch at him, saying, "Here's half of this to you, Captain Graves!"

The Virginia captain, overwhelmed by his misfortune, excused himself from drinking with Low. Whereupon the pirate cocked his pistol threateningly at his captive, saying, "Either take one or the other, Captain."

Poor Graves was forced to drink until he collapsed on the deck.

Low's cruelty was equaled only by his luck capturing ships. His next prize was a vessel called the *Christmas*. Mounting her with 34 guns, he dubbed himself her admiral, and when he saw a brigantine approaching he hoisted the black flag. The ship's crew, seeing the formidable display of guns facing them from the gunwales, immediately surrendered. Half the men were English and half Portuguese. The Portuguese seamen Low despised, and he hanged them all, but the English he thrust into a small boat with a curse and sent them off into the open sea, setting their vessel afire behind them. His crew, leaning upon the rails, gestured at the unfortunate seamen and laughed uproariously.

But all wickedness ends at last. Finally, Low overstepped his cruelty even among the crew of the *Christmas* by murdering his own quartermaster as the man lay asleep in his bunk. At this, the crew rose against him. They carried the struggling Captain Low to a boat, which they shoved off without any provisions, abandoning him to the fate they hoped would end his life.

Edward Low had time for a great deal of thinking as he drifted at sea in the boat. His mother back in England—would he ever see her again? It had been several years since he had gone home. His reputation had spread, and he might be recognized on the docks of Westminster. But not long after he was cast adrift, his usual good luck prevailed. A French vessel happened along and picked him up. He began a dramatic recital.

"My crew mutinied, and then they abandoned me when I tried to keep them from turning to piracy," he said righteously.

"He's lying," shouted a man among the crew. "He's Captain Edward Low!"

Startled, Low looked up from telling his story and into the speaker's face. He saw a tall fellow with a rawboned face tanned to a dark mahogany hue. Something about him was familiar as the dark-blue eyes of an Englishman stared back ironically into his. Low's face paled beneath his badly sunburned skin.

Lest there be any doubt, the man cried out, "What mercy did you have for the French cook when you tied him to the mast and set his ship aflame?"

"What better identification do we need?" said the French captain.

"No! No!" Low cried out as the captain ordered him put in irons. "Mercy . . . have mercy!"

But the hearts of the crew were hardened against the man they had pitied only minutes before. All were familiar with stories of his disgusting cruelties. Changing the ship's course and sailing into Martinique, the French captain handed him over to the authorities, who, after a quick trial, hanged Edward Low on a specially erected gallows.

"You monster!" said the man who had identified him as he stood before the scaffold. Edward Low looked coldly into the face of his own brother.

Lewis Guittar
Virginia to West Indies

L ewis Guittar was small-boned but muscular, with the courage of a tiger. An adventurous, resourceful man, almost totally without fear, he had everything he needed to be a successful pirate— everything but a decent ship instead of the tiny, unseaworthy sloop he was now sailing. It was December of 1699, and Captain Guittar had no idea that in a few months he would not only have a ship to be proud of, but would be on his way to making history in the pirate annals of North America. The place: Chesapeake Bay.

The newly elected captain had been in command less than two weeks, and he stalked about his vessel, cursing her sometimes in French, sometimes Spanish—her size, her slowness. Setting sail from Ponte a Gravois, in the West Indies, as he cruised the coast of Hispaniola he was fortunate enough to seize a small Dutch trader laden with linen. After plundering her of part of her cargo and all the brandy, he let her and the crew go—with the exception of the surgeon. A good doctor was handy for removing bullets and stitching cutlass wounds, but this man was to prove immensely valuable in a most unexpected way.

Claiming that he had been cheated out of 700 gold crowns by a

Captain Cornelius Isaac, master of a Dutch merchant ship, the surgeon could not cease praising Isaac's ship to the skies—"such a fine vessel, superb sailing qualities." Gradually, in his mind's eye, Guittar began to see this ship as his own, and the surgeon, eager for revenge, encouraged him.

"When I take her, I promise to set this man who has cheated you— this rascal, Captain Isaac, adrift," promised Guittar, excited at the prospect of owning such a swift vessel.

The doctor smiled his satisfaction. "You will find her at the Saltitudos." (Ile de la Tortue is the modern-day name.)

The ship, named *La Paix* (ironically, *The Peace*), was right where the surgeon had said. Guittar took her with a swift surprise attack and was about to put Isaac and some crew members off in a boat when one of Isaac's crew, a Dutchman named Houghling whom Guittar was taking with him, pleaded to be given a "tickett," saying that he was innocent of piracy and had been forced.

Isaac, captain of the captured vessel, was surprised but agreeable, and before he was set adrift by Guittar he was allowed to sit down at the table in the cabin, where he wrote out a clear statement declaring:

> John Houghling is forced against his will to stay and remane upon the Ship LaPaix under the Command of Lewis Guittar and have set our hands to winess it to ye and no body should trouble him or should pretend he was there by his own consent. Witness our hands
> Cornelius Isaac.

Guittar now had the ship of his dreams. *La Paix* weighed 200 tons, was 84 feet long and 25 wide, and had a single deck fore and aft. Above the single deck was a small forecastle and a half deck extended to the mainmast. He estimated that 20 iron guns on carriages could be mounted on her, which would make this ship a formidable force in battle.

Thirty-eight men from another pirate ship joined them, and from here and there along the coast of Hispaniola Guittar picked up castaways and shipwreck victims until his crew numbered about 125 men. As they made their way north toward the American coast they swelled their crew with additional recruits from the coast of Cuba and the Gulf.

Before leaving Cuban waters on April 17, 1700, they met the pink *Baltimore*. The vessel was about half the size of *La Paix* and a highly maneuverable and fast sailer, faster even than Guittar's own ship. Quickly hoisting Dutch colors, Guittar pretended that he was in distress. Captain Lovejoy, master of the pink *Baltimore*, waited to see if he could assist the other vessel. Raising his hand in a friendly fashion, Guittar hailed him as they drew alongside; then, without warning, he fired a shot, killing one of the ship's passengers.

It was too late for Lovejoy to correct his mistake, and soon several of his crew lay bound as prisoners in the pirate's hold. Deciding to make the *Baltimore* a consort of *La Paix*, Guittar sent his own quartermaster and ten crewmen aboard with instructions to steer a course along with them for Virginia and take anything they could on the way. A meeting place in the Capes was selected in the event they became separated.

Captain Guittar looked forward to this cruise into the Chesapeake. The heat was considerably less than in the tropics, and his little flotilla could make needed repairs and take on water. He was less than 100 leagues from Virginia when his consort, the *Baltimore*, captured another ship, the *George*, bound from Philadelphia to Jamaica. They took her crew off and imprisoned them aboard *La Paix*, but they did not consider the ship worth saving, so they bored a hole in her side, set the cabin afire and sank her.

Only 30 leagues from their destination of Cape Henry, Virginia, the pirate ships sighted the *Barbados Merchant*—a plump little brigantine and a nice addition to their small fleet. Both ships began to pursue her, but the *Baltimore* speedily left Guittar's ship behind, overtaking and capturing the brigantine. They wrecked the *Barbados Merchant*, cutting away bowsprit, masts, sails and rigging and breaking her compass before abandoning her. Her master, Captain Fletcher, was fortunately able to retrieve and use some of the rigging that had been left dangling over the side, and, finding an old compass, he managed to steer the limping brigantine into Accomac.

Meanwhile, the pirate pink, *Baltimore*, arriving at the Capes, was just in time to take the *Wheeler* as it emerged from the York River. After plundering her, the pirates cut a hole in her bottom and sunk her. Then the *Baltimore* spied another brigantine about eight miles south of Cape Henry. With wild shouts and waving cutlasses, they boarded and looted her. Though stripped of sails and mast and with her rudder cut off, this brig would also manage to get back to the Capes and give the alarm.

Guittar came up just after the plundering had taken place and flashed a light for the pink to follow. She ignored it and went her merry way. It was the last the angry Captain Guittar would ever see of the *Baltimore* with his greedy quartermaster and ten crewmen. But he was to sight his own big prize the next day.

Captain Samuel Harrison's brigantine, the *Pennsylvania Merchant*, on its way from England to Philadelphia, lay becalmed about 80 miles off Cape Henry. That morning, just as Harrison was standing in for shore, the wind had died. He paced the deck with frustration but soon gave it up and settled himself in his cabin to wait. It was not until early in the afternoon that the wind began to move the sails slightly. At just about the same time, Harrison saw a ship flying the Dutch colors with a small sloop alongside. He could not know that these ships belonged to the pirate Guittar—who had added the small sloop to his ranks in place of the disloyal *Baltimore*—but he knew enough to be wary when he noticed that the two ships were trying to get windward of him. Suspicious, he outmaneuvered them. As the *Pennsylvania Merchant* sailed north, he realized the two pirate vessels were not far behind. Passing the ravaged *Barbados Merchant* limping into port at Accomac, he stopped briefly to jury-rig her foremast but, in flight himself, he had no time to help her further.

Dusk was beginning to fall when Guittar overtook him and

shouted across, "Strike your colors!"

"Keep off or I will fire!" Harrison called back boldly.

There was no reply from the dark ship lying nearby. Guittar had decided not to make a boarding attempt in the dark. He could wait. At dawn the *Pennsylvania Merchant* and the pirate vessels were in close range of each other and Captain Harrison saw that the larger of the pirate ships was much bigger than he had realized.

"Strike your colors," Guittar barked impatiently, and this time he waved to his crew to fire with their pistols. The gunfire had the desired effect, for the *Pennsylvania Merchant* immediately lowered her flag.

Commanding Captain Harrison to come on board, Guittar asked, "Why did you not strike your colors sooner?"

"Because there was peace with all the world," Harrison replied naively. It seemed that with the end of privateering, he really had not considered the possibility of pirates.

Small boats began going back and forth between the ships while the pirates systematically robbed crew and passengers and loaded the loot into the boats. The lading of goods, worth more than 3,000 pounds, was immediately carried aboard, and nothing escaped Captain Guittar's attention, including the *Merchant's* sails and rigging, which he ordered his men to strip from the ship and store on *La Paix*.

Harrison watched all this with despair, realizing that Guittar planned to destroy his ship, and he began to plead with the pirates, not sensitive to their rising irritation and the violence he might provoke. Several crewmen told him he was lucky, for when certain other ships had resisted, they had hanged men from the yardarm. But Harrison continued to plead, and finally, after nearly two days of plundering and loading cargo, Guittar put the ship's fate to a vote. The vote was to burn her. The Frenchman considered this decision common sense, not malice, for anyone returning to port on the ship surely would have notified Virginia authorities.

John Houghling, the pilot of *La Paix*, built a raging fire in the cabin, and another pirate forced the ship's carpenter to cut a hole in the side of the vessel to sink her. Houghling's early protests over being forced into piracy had vanished with the pirate's successes, and he and Captain Guittar were now fast friends.

Back on board *La Paix*, the pirates divided the piles of plunder and began their celebration. They danced about the deck, two-stepping, shimmying and skipping awkwardly until they fell here and there in a stupor from strong drink. "A Rejoycing for the Success they had in their Villanies," said one of the pirates later.

Early on the morning of April 28, Guittar saw two merchant vessels leaving the Chesapeake about fifteen miles from Cape Henry. One was the beautiful *Indian King*, built in Virginia, bound for London and commanded by Captain Edward Whitaker. This vessel immediately appealed to Guittar, and he started after it. He managed to come quite close, for the captain of the *Indian King* took the pirates to be honest men and thought he might have company on at least part of his voyage. Within a short distance of Whitaker, Guittar hoisted a Dutch ensign briefly and then ran up the red pirate flag. He fired a shot at the other ship. It was now too late for Captain Whitaker, and he struck his colors.

A boatload of pirates boarded the *Indian King* and took their mate, surgeon, crew and passengers, as well as Whitaker, over to the buccaneers' ship. There they were robbed and then imprisoned below deck. As he questioned the captain, Guittar asked whether any men-of-war were protecting the Chesapeake. To his delight, Whitaker knew of none and told him so.

It was mid-morning when *La Paix* attacked the smaller ship that had accompanied the *Indian King*, and the pirates fired upon the crew. At the first volley, the captain fell to the deck, covered with blood. The mate was ordered aboard, and Guittar dispatched four of his men to take command.

"Was anyone mortally wounded?" Guittar asked the mate, Calwell.

"One man," replied he.

"Who?" questioned Captain Guittar.

"The master."

"I can send our surgeon over," offered Guittar, who seemed genuinely sorry. "There may be some hope for him."

"It's too late."

"Oh, what a shame," spoke up Houghling with feigned sympathy. "And where was he standing?"

"By the mizzen shroud."

"No," corrected Houghling. "He was by the mizzenmast, and I fired the gun that shot him." He burst into a fit of wild laughter.

The pirates entered Chesapeake Bay towing their captured ships and saw several vessels at anchor. One of them, the *Nicholson*, which had been ready to leave port, tried to flee although constantly under fire from the pirates. Her mainyard and topsail were both shot away before the master, Robert Lurtine, would surrender her. As Lurtine boarded *La Paix*, Guittar did not notice a tiny pink slipping swiftly into the James River. He did not know her captain was taking word to the Virginia authorities of his activities.

Soon after boarding Lurtine's ship, the pirates discovered large quantities of beer and red wine and began drinking heavily while they celebrated. As they drank, they became more cruel, beating the *Nicholson*'s crew with the flats of their cutlasses and flogging them brutally with tarred rope ends. One of Guittar's own men who had been forced broke down and cried at the brutal whipping the other buccaneers were giving the *Nicholson*'s gunner. Eventually Guittar put a stop to some of the cruelty—not because he cared for the victims, but because he needed his men to get busy transferring cargo. The work proceeded, but at an ever slowing pace, for the pirates were collapsing into a drunken stupor.

Meanwhile at Kiquotan, Virginia, Captain William Passenger, commander of the British vessel *Shoreham*, was paying his respects to Governor Nicholson when the news of pirates' presence arrived with the ship that had escaped Guittar's notice in Chesapeake Bay. Captain Passenger bounded from his chair, ready to go to the *Shoreham* immediately and set out in pursuit of the pirates. The governor urged him to wait until morning, but when he saw Passenger would not heed his advice, he boarded the ship himself along with the British captain, and the *Shoreham* set sail. Unfortunately the wind was against them so that they made little progress, and as night approached they were forced to anchor about 12 miles from the pirate vessel.

Captain Whitaker, a prisoner on board *La Paix*, saw the *Shoreham* next morning coming into the bay. He told Guittar that she was a great ship.

"But you said no man-of-war was in Virginia waters," protested Guittar.

"The *Essex* left the harbor to be careened. They must be replacing it."

"It's likely a merchantman, and I will take him," Guittar said boastfully, for his confidence in his own ability never flagged.

Captain Passenger had set sail just before sunrise, and by four in the afternoon he was within half a mile of Guittar. When the pirate captain saw the great Royal Navy ship, there was no doubt in his mind that he was confronting a man-of-war. Some pirates might have fled, but not the bold Frenchman. Up went a large, blood-red pennant.

Passenger fired a broadside, commanding him to surrender, but Guittar's only response was to return the fire.

The commander of the *Shoreham* was an expert sailor and anticipated that the pirates would try to bring their vessel to windward and board him. He kept steadily to windward of the pirate ship and was fortunate in having a gale blowing which favored this position. At the same time he kept up a furious fire. Passenger's crew was not what he would have wished. Some were mere boys. But the superior firepower began to have its effect, and the two ships—within pistol shot of each other—battled fiercely.

On the beach at Lynnhaven Bay, a large crowd of spectators stood watching, for sounds of the battle could be heard as far as Point Comfort.

The fearless Guittar was everywhere, leading his men, and pilot John Houghling was shouting above the din, "We'll soon get windward and have the dogs!"

Down in the hold of *La Paix*, prisoners from the captured ships listened tensely to the gunfire and sounds of battle. Some dared to steal an occasional look above, where one volley of shot after another whistled past. The deck was strewn with dead and wounded. Now and then one of the pirates would reach down with blood-streaked arms and throw several bodies overboard—not knowing whether he was lofting the dead or the merely wounded, but frustrated with the human obstacles everywhere about him. Faced with dying at the hands of the enemy or hanging, Lewis Guittar fought on. The masts and rigging of *La Paix* were shattered by shot, its hull nearly blasted to pieces. He brought his ship about, and although she was being swept by small shot, he still would not surrender. The two ships had now battled for ten hours.

On the *Shoreham* Governor Nicholson himself fought heroically, but Captain Passenger was responsible for giving orders to his inexperienced crew and directing the attack. He would later be cited for his courage.

Aware that the contest was nearing an end, Guittar ordered Houghling to bring the ship about and drive *La Paix* ashore—not easy since her rudder had been shot off. The ship lurched heavily, throwing everyone about as she drove aground. On deck Captain Guittar struck his colors, and both sides ceased firing. The *Shoreham* did not realize that Guittar was buying time.

Now the pirates hurried to place a trail of gunpowder across their deck, linking it to 30 barrels of explosives in order to blow up the ship. They had agreed to live and to die together.

Appearing in the hold, Captain Guittar announced to his prisoners, "I am going to blow up this ship, and we will all die together." The prisoners were terrified.

"Wait! Let one of us swim to the *Shoreham* and bargain instead as to how they will deal with you and your men," argued Captain Lurtine. One of the captives agreed to go. He jumped into the water, but betrayed his fellow captives by swimming to shore and escaping.

Then, John Lumpany, a man who had been a passenger on the *Pennsylvania Merchant*, approached Guittar. His nervousness must have been apparent, for to his surprise the captain of the pirates reassured him.

"Be of good courage," Lewis Guittar said. "Tell the commander in chief if he will not give me and my men quarter and pardon, I will blow up this ship and we will all die together."

Lurtine swam to the *Shoreham* and relayed the terms.

Governor Nicholson wrote this reply, taking the trouble to render *La Paix* in sarcastic misspelling:

> Whereas Captain Lewis [sic] Commander of the Lay Past hath preferred to surrender himselfe, men and ship together with what effects thereunto belongeth provided he may have quarter which I grant him on performance of the same and referr him and his men to the mercy of my Royal Master King William the third whom God preserve.

Better a chance for life than the certainty of death, thought the pirate chieftain, staring at the trail of powder across a deck that seemed to have been painted scarlet with blood. He enjoyed living as much as the next man, and he was having second thoughts about them all dying together. The king's *mercy*, the note had said. It might give them a chance.

He accepted the terms.

The buccaneers had fought off the man-of-war from early morning until three that afternoon when they surrendered the remains of *La Paix*. From Virginia, captain and crew were sent in irons to London, where Guittar and 60 crewmen were tried. The crew and Guittar himself were convicted and hanged on November 23, 1700.

When the sentence was pronounced the merest trace of a sardonic smile crossed Captain Lewis Guittar's face. Though Nicholson's note had promised to refer him and his men "to the mercy of my Royal

Majesty King William," he was not really surprised when the king failed to show mercy.

For wasn't that often the case on his own ship?

William Lewis

Virginia to Carolina to Florida to West Indies

T he boy's stomach was beginning to turn over now, and he knew
   he would get sick if he did not stop staring at the limp figure
hanging from the yardarm. The dead man's trousers fluttered in the
wind, and the body swayed slightly when the ship rocked from the
swell. It was dusk, but work still continued around the boy on the
dock. No one else seemed disturbed by the ghastly presence; pirates'
bodies hanging in the harbor were not an uncommon sight.

During the years Billy Lewis had sailed with Banister, he had
known his benefactor was a pirate. He has also known that pirates
were hanged if caught, but the danger had never been real to him
until Banister's ship had been captured by a British man-of-war and
the men brought into harbor at Jamaica for trial.

"Young scoundrels!" the English seaman had called him and his
friend, Darby McCaffrey, and with ropes around their middles he had
brought them into the island port dangling uncomfortably from the
mizzen peak. Remembering, Billy rubbed his hand ruefully over the
still-raw place around his belly.

He couldn't keep from looking at the figure of Banister, his former
friend, dressed in white shirt and striped pants. The moon came out,

illuminating the head hanging downward and tilted slightly to one side. Billy would have recognized Banister in hell itself, he thought. For a moment he wondered if his old friend *was* in hell. Lord! He hoped not. And then there was a faint sound behind him.

"*An ugly death for you . . . you, too,*" he thought he heard a voice saying over the lapping of the water. He shivered and turned quickly, but no one was there. The dock was almost empty of men.

The pirate Banister had been kind to the boy, taking far more interest in him than his old man. Billy had frequented the docks of Boston from the time he was eight or nine years old, and he knew most of the pirates and admired them. Banister protected him from those he said were "a bad sort," teased him, and now and then bought him drinks in waterfront pubs. By the time he was ten Billy knew that he was going to be a pirate, too. He had a way of just knowing the things that were going to happen to him.

A year later he persuaded Banister to take him to sea. The pirate told everyone he was his nephew, and on shipboard Billy was under his wing. Of course, after all of them were captured, Billy told the English officers he and Darby had been "impressed," taken against their will—he knew enough to say that—and the officers let them go free.

They were hired on a ship out of Jamaica a month later. It was a legitimate cargo ship, and Billy liked the master, who proved to be a decent sort. He seemed to take to Billy, too, giving him a turn at the wheel now and then and going to some trouble to teach him about sailing. They sailed together for almost five years.

One day a ship loomed on the horizon, and the master hailed it. The sloop had a large crew, and men lined the rail. The master hailed them again. The only reply was the hoisting of the black flag in the breeze and a broadside from one of their guns.

Within minutes, Spanish pirates had thrown a hawser over the rail and boarded the cargo ship. It was useless to offer resistance, for the cargo ship had only two rail-mounted guns loaded with small shot. Because of his years at sea with crewmen from many countries, Billy spoke English, French, and fluent Spanish and was soon conversing with the pirates. The Spaniards set sail for Havana, and when they arrived, they celebrated for days. Darby was something of a ballad singer, always in demand, and the boys were popular, enjoying the gaiety and entertainment of Havana harbor life. Conditions on shipboard, however, were not to their liking.

"I'd as soon be a slave," said Billy, and Darby nodded his agreement. At the first opportunity they were joined by six like-minded Spaniards and ran off with a small canoe. Lewis at sixteen had grown into a sturdy young fellow with a mane of thick, wavy black hair and a commanding personality. Under his leadership the group surprised and took a Spanish piragua. Two of the men from that ship joined Lewis. Now they were ten, Bill Lewis in command. He soon surprised a turtling sloop and took several of the hands with him. And so it went—Lewis in the piragua, surprising turtle sloops and forcing some to sign on with him until finally he had built a company of about 40 men.

Then he saw a ship better suited to his purpose, a large pink, a narrow-sterned, swift ship bound from Jamaica to the bay of Campeachy. Capturing the vessel, he heard from one of the crew that out in the bay sailed a well-built brigantine of ten guns, commanded by a Captain Tucker.

He sent Tucker an ultimatum, telling him the ship was just what he wanted. He offered to pay Tucker 10,000 pieces-of-eight for the vessel. If he refused to sell her, Lewis threatened to lie in wait and take her by force. He was determined to have the ship. Captain Tucker read the letter, signed *Captain William Lewis*, and sent for the masters of the other vessels lying in the bay—about ten sloops in all.

Showing them the letter, Tucker said, "This Lewis is a pirate and a danger to all of us. Send me about five men from each of your vessels to reinforce my men," he urged, "and I'll go out and fight him."

The masters shifted in their chairs and looked at each other dubiously.

"We can't hazard our own men," they protested. "We're good

sailors, and each of us can take care of himself."

Tucker was unable to convince them of their peril alone in the face of this threat, and they all put to sea, Tucker among them. They had not sailed far when, near land, they spied a sail which had a breeze while they lay becalmed. Some thought the sail belonged to a turtler, but Tucker and others were convinced it was the pirate. It was.

In order to move more swiftly among them than the wind would allow, Lewis also used oars and was soon in their midst. The sloops were easy prey for him, having only two to four guns each—or no guns at all. Even at this late moment Tucker exhorted the others to send him men to lead a fight, but they didn't respond. About that time a breeze came up, and, seeing the other masters would not support him, Tucker trimmed his sails, heading swiftly for the open sea, firing a broadside into the pirate ship as he passed. The other ships all fell prey to Captain Lewis.

A vessel whose master was a very good sailor was trying to slip away when he was stopped by one shot from Lewis. This sloop then lay by until the rest were all visited and taken. Lewis sent aboard and ordered the master into his sloop.

"What was the reason for your lying by and betraying your owners' trust?" said he. "Your vessel is a much faster one than mine, and you could easily have gotten away." Captain Lewis picked up a rope end and fell to striking the man. "You dishonest coward. I'm going to punish you!" he cried out. Dropping the rope, he seized a cane and drove the ship's master about the deck.

Thinking to placate Captain Lewis, the master said, "There is plenty of money on board my ship, and I'll show you where it is."

"You villain for betraying your owners!" Lewis shouted, redoubling his blows with the cane—but he also sent over to the master's ship, taking the money from the vessel as well as 40 able-bodied black seamen and a white carpenter. This task completed, he appropriated for himself the largest sloop, which was about 90 feet long. He mounted her with 12 guns and christened her the *Morning Star*, telling himself that it was his symbol.

His crew was now 80 strong. With the confidence these numbers gave him, William Lewis and his old friend, quartermaster Darby, cruised the Gulf of Florida, plundering several ships.

Then they headed for the coast of Carolina. Near Charles Towne they found the natives glad to trade for rum and sugar. The big sloop was not as fast as she might have been, for she needed her hull cleaned, and Lewis was lucky enough to come upon a secluded creek not too distant from the city. But he was on guard so that he would not be surprised from the shore. Here a great many men, whom the pirates had forced, ran away and managed to blend into the population of the city of Charles Towne, some settling there.

Lewis cleaned his sloop speedily before the authorities could learn of his presence. Thinking it wise to leave the area for a time, he made a brief foray up to Virginia, plundering several merchant ships as he went, before returning to Carolina. Once more the *Morning Star* lay off the coast near Charles Towne. Lewis continued boldly capturing and plundering vessels. These raids provided fresh produce, meat, rum and a generous amount of booty, and the crew would have been content with their shares had it not been for friction between the English crewmen and the French.

Most of the Frenchmen had joined Lewis willingly, but many of the Englishmen had been forced. Captain Lewis soon overheard from unguarded bits of the Englishmen's conversation that they planned to maroon him and the Frenchmen. He and Darby lost no time spreading this news among the French. In the early morning hours Lewis and his loyal men struck, setting upon all the suspected plotters and shoving them into a boat. Although they desperately implored him not to leave them out there, Lewis ordered them given ten pieces of beef and set their boat adrift ten miles from shore. Some of the blacks and the Frenchmen thought he should find an island where ships might pass and maroon the suspects there, but Lewis was angry, and he was listening to another voice—almost inaudible, but persistent.

"Leave them in the boat. They'll die . . . die . . ." the voice

reverberated. And then the words came more distinctly: "*Die like you.*" He looked over his shoulder and felt foolish for doing so, for his crew were on their way to the galley and he was alone. But the words resounded over and over, even when he covered his ears and fled to his cabin, where he fell upon his bunk and finally slept.

Leaving Carolina for the banks of Newfoundland, Captain Billy Lewis sailed into Trinity Harbor in Conception Bay, where he seized a 24-gun galley called the *Herman*, one of several vessels under the command of Captain Woodes Rogers. Rogers, who was ashore, told Lewis that if he would send quartermaster Darby ashore, the masters of the other vessels would furnish the pirates with supplies. But when Darby came ashore, the other masters held a meeting and decided that instead they would seize the quartermaster. They took Darby McCaffrey to Rogers, who brutally chained him to the sheet anchor—a rope at the lower corners of a sail—which was on shore. Then the masters of the ships planted guns at the point to prevent the pirate getting away. Someone accidentally fired one of the guns, and the noise alerted William Lewis that the ship masters were deceiving him.

Under cover of darkness Lewis sailed the *Herman* out of Trinity Harbor, although not undamaged, for the vessels began shooting at him. Lewis swore he would not leave the harbor entrance until he got his quartermaster back, but the masters would not release Darby. Soon Captain Lewis intercepted two fishing boats, and on one was lucky enough to find the brother of the *Herman*'s galley captain. Lewis now sent word that if his quartermaster were not immediately returned he would put to death not only the brother of the galley captain but all the rest of the prisoners from the two fishing shallops as well.

At this threat Darby was sent back to Lewis without delay. The pirate asked Darby how he had been treated, and he replied, "Very courteously."

"That's well," said Lewis, speaking in French to conceal his remarks from Darby's English captors. "If you had been mistreated, I would have put all these rascals to the sword."

The *Herman* galley captain's brother went over to the rail, and Darby stopped him, saying loudly that when he returned to his ship, he must drink to all the masters' health, particularly that of Captain Rogers. Then he quickly whispered in the man's ear that if Lewis knew he had been chained all night to the sheet anchor, he and all his fellow crew would be cut to pieces. The man's face blanched. After he and the other fishermen had all boarded their fishing boats, quartermaster McCaffrey told Lewis how he had really been treated. The captain was furious.

McCaffrey let him rage for awhile and finally said, "I'm sorry, sir. I didn't think the innocent should suffer for the guilty." Lewis's eyes met his, and then he pressed his lips together in a tight angry line, sighed and nodded agreement.

Whether from the pressure of thoughts that had lain submerged for a long time, or from fatigue from his ordeal of the night before, Darby went on, "We've been lucky for many years, *mon capitan*, and we have much money. What would you think of our leaving this sort of life?"

Lewis looked astonished. "Leave the sea—the adventure of it?" For a moment his eyes held the same fire Darby had seen so many times when they were side by side scrambling over a ship's gunwales with drawn swords. "What other challenge could there be?"

"To find a different sort of life and lead it with the same excitement you have found in this one."

William Lewis's face softened for a moment as he listened to his old friend, and then he stared out toward the horizon. With a leonine gesture he shook the black locks from his face, and there was a hint of sadness in his dark eyes.

"I'll think about it, Darby. The pull of this life for me has been like strong drink for some men, but after a time the drink no longer brings the same satisfaction."

The masters of the merchant vessels immediately reported their encounter with Lewis to the captain of a man-of-war at St. John's. He was under sail immediately but was four hours behind the pirates. Meanwhile Lewis kept within sight of the coast, taking several French and English merchant ships, until he decided to put into harbor. Here Darby pointed out a French vessel, and Lewis coveted her the moment he saw her. She mounted 24 guns.

"I'd say that vessel was built near the end of the war for a privateer," observed the pirate captain, admiring her through his glasses, his eyes bright.

"She's out here to protect those two fishing boats," Darby commented. "Bound to have speed." The two men's eyes met.

The commander of the ship hailed them. "We're from Jamaica with rum and sugar," replied Lewis.

The French commander shouted for them to go about their business. "There's a pirate sloop on the coast," he warned, "and I might think you're the rogue yourself, if you don't sheer off right away. Otherwise I'll fire a broadside into you."

William Lewis shouted his thanks, sheered off hurriedly and went out to sea—but just far enough not to be visible from shore. The Frenchman, not so sure the pirate vessel was gone and being on his guard, raised a battery of guns on shore overlooking the harbor.

Sending out a small boat now and then to reconnoiter, Darby had his doubts about their ability to endure the fire from the battery lining the harbor while at the same time seizing a 24-gun ship. He warned Lewis that they might sacrifice a good many of their men trying, but the captain, lost in thought, didn't seem to hear him. *Maybe I'm becoming a nervous old lady*, thought Darby, knitting the thick blond brows that now had a touch of gray. *I'm certainly not as reckless as I used to be.*

The pirates stayed anchored at sea. While the crew muttered, William Lewis paced the deck, swore sometimes under his breath and rejected one plan of action after another. Finally he had it!

Two weeks after he had left the harbor, when he was thought to be long gone, Lewis returned. It was shortly after midnight. Suddenly seizing the two fishing shallops belonging to the Frenchman, Lewis split his crew and manned the two boats with his pirates. With Darby commanding one boat and Lewis the other, they entered the harbor. The crew of Darby's boat attacked the guns lining the harbor. After a few minutes of quiet, a semi-circle of shore guns spat fire. Darby protected his boat as much as possible, knowing that although the aim was inaccurate from that distance, a lucky shot could sink them or at the very least kill someone.

The other boat, commanded by Lewis himself, stormed the gunwales of the former privateer, surprising and capturing it. Just as the battle ended, William Lewis saw the morning star appear. Remembering his old ship by that name, Lewis knew how he would christen his new prize.

"You're wanting our liquor, I suppose," said the French captain to the pirate captain as they met each other.

"I want your ship," retorted Lewis in French, his sword still in hand.

The Frenchman saw that Lewis meant it and accepted defeat philosophically, ordering his crew to trim the sails. Lewis gave him his sloop and all the fish his men had caught, except for some that he took as provisions for his own crew. The crew of the defeated vessel, some of whom were beginning to shout, "Voilà! Voilà!" obviously admired the pirate. Several signed on with him. By force or voluntarily, the captain now had 200 men.

But the victory did not contain the thrill Lewis had expected, for the other shallop had been struck by shore artillery and Darby was dead. Lewis felt sad, and more than a little bitter—the finest vessel they had ever captured, and Darby McCaffrey would not be here to sail it with him.

From then on he seemed to drink more and behave with a greater recklessness.

A strange circumstance occurred while he was off the coast of Carolina in chase of a vessel. His fore and main top-mast were carried away, and Lewis, running up the shrouds to the main-top, tore out a handful of his hair. Casting it to the wind, he shouted, "Good Devil, take this till I come!" Afterwards the men who heard him noticed that their ship sailed faster in the chase than before the loss of the top-masts. Did they have a satanic ally? They wondered and were afraid.

Lewis's behavior became peculiar in other ways. He took a Captain Smith's ship and treated him very courteously, giving him as much, if not more, in value than he took from him. Releasing Smith, Lewis said he would come to Carolina after he had made more money and would rely on Smith's friendship. It was plain that the captain missed Darby; perhaps he was thinking that if taking the French vessel had not become an obsession with him, Darby would still be alive. Perhaps he now saw that there was more to life than he had realized, and that somehow he had lost what he valued most.

After Lewis had stayed on the Carolina coast for several weeks, the inevitable happened. The French and the English crewmen began quarreling and decided to part. The French selected a ship, elected a man named Le Barre captain and left, but Lewis was angry and had been drinking. He caught up with them, marooned some and took back a handful of the others including Le Barre. That night all of the men drank heavily.

The blacks on board, still loyal to Captain Lewis, went to him. "Sir, the French have a plot against you. We must get ready."

He stared back at the men for a long time without speaking. At last he said simply, "I cannot withstand my destiny." The men were bewildered.

"Here in my cabin," Lewis went on, "the Devil spoke to me, saying that I'll be murdered tonight." The blacks shrank back in fear at the mention of the Devil. Lewis's eyes were wild and dark, and his face had the look of a man who has already left the land of the living. In a sense he had, for during the night the rest of the marooned French found canoes and came back. They boarded the *Morning Star*, and by an ironic circumstance, this time the star's rising did not bring Lewis good luck. The French murdered him in his bed.

And just as William Lewis had said, the words of the Devil were his destiny.

John Quelch
New England to South America

"This should make you a wealthy man," said the governor. "Be sure to observe your instructions, captain," he warned and then dismissed him with a courteous nod.

It was July of 1703 when Captain Daniel Plowman bade good-bye to Governor Joseph Dudley, holding in his hand the permission of the governor of Massachusetts Bay and New Hampshire to "Arm, Furnish and Equip the said Brigantine in Warlike manner, against Her Majestie's said Enemies," and an authorization to "War, Fight, Take, Kill, Suppress and Destroy any pirates, Privateers, or other Subjects and Vassals of France or Spain, the declared enemies of the Crown of England."

A new 80-ton craft, the *Charles*, had already been fitted out by leading citizens of Boston as a privateer to prey upon French shipping off the coast of Acadia (today's Nova Scotia) and Newfoundland. She was to bring whatever she captured into the port of Boston if the vessel was in the vicinity. Plowman foresaw a highly profitable future, for privateering was a thriving business. Unfortunately, there were other circumstances that he had not foreseen.

He frowned, his eyes returning to the ridiculous warning at the beginning of his instructions. He was not to allow his crew to swear or get drunk? He realized drunkenness could create a serious problem, but who knew any seamen who didn't swear or sometimes get drunk? It tired him just to read this foolishness. In fact, he had felt under the weather for the past month, which was why he had placed the responsibility of hiring the crew in the hands of his lieutenant commander, a 38-year-old Englishman named John Quelch. Now, for the life of him, he could not recall who had recommended Quelch.

"Be sure to hire only men of upright character," he had told Quelch. "Reject any rascals."

"Of course, sir," Quelch had replied reassuringly. Thus had Plowman's ill fortune begun.

The captain had spent the following fortnight resting at his home. Only this week, when he had taken his belongings to his cabin on the *Charles*, did Plowman notice the appearance of his crew members. A brutal, shifty-eyed lot they were. Just to look at these men brought to his mind another privateer, Captain Kidd, and his ship, the *Adventure Galley*. Plowman became apprehensive. Some believed that Kidd's fate the year before was due to his ship being taken over by a crew of ruffians. Gazing around the *Charles*, the captain thought he had never seen men who appeared such rascals.

Shortly after leaving Boston his illness took a turn for the worse, weakening him considerably, and Plowman decided to write the owners in Boston. He expressed alarm at the character of his crew and requested that the owners come to Marblehead Harbor, north of Boston, where the ship was anchoring, to "take speedy care in saving what we can."

"The captain is too sick to talk to you," one owner who did go was told, and he was not allowed to see Captain Plowman. On his return, the owners held a meeting and decided to get a new captain as soon as they could, but they did not act on this resolve.

Summoning all his strength, Plowman then wrote a desperate

plea, begging the owners to bring the *Charles* back to Boston and get all guns and supplies ashore before it was too late. "It will not do with these people," he warned, referring again to his fears about the crew. Once more the owners did nothing—and their inactivity sealed the captain's fate.

Plowman was lying sick in his bunk when he heard footsteps approaching, then stopping outside his cabin. Then came the sound of a hammer's loud pounding. Plowman staggered weakly to the door, jerked at it and discovered, to his horror, that it had been nailed shut from the other side.

The door had been nailed closed on the orders of quartermaster Anthony Holding. It was the first step in his nefarious plot.

Going up on deck, Holding sent New Englander John Lambert, who knew Boston, ashore to summon Lieutenant Commander Quelch. Like many officers, Quelch had chosen to stay in town while the ship was in its home port. Within the hour John Quelch came aboard, and at a hurriedly assembled meeting presided over by Holding, he found himself elected captain. Once again his knack for choosing his associates had brought him luck, thought Quelch. More than once, just in associating with smart people some of their success seemed to rub off on him and he didn't have to take any risks. Holding was smart and shrewd, and Quelch had guessed his intentions from the start.

As the brigantine *Charles* left Marblehead Harbor, Quelch tossed a penny on the barnacle encrusted "Halfway Rock." "Just for good luck, Tony," he said to Holding.

"The only kind of good luck I believe in will be when you see that our friend below deck is at the bottom of the sea!" said Holding, with a meaningful look. Then the dark shape of the *Charles* slipped past Cat Island on her way out to sea.

Some crew members later claimed that the captain had been murdered, while others maintained that he had died of his illness. A more likely scenario is that when the *Charles* was safely out of the harbor, a half-dozen men, acting under the orders of Holding, pulled Captain Plowman from his bunk and tossed him over the rail into Boston Bay.

As the ship anchored in various ports, Quelch, upon Holding's advice, made no effort to contact the Boston ship owners or reassure them about the vessel's sudden departure. The owners of the *Charles*, awaiting information as to the progress of their venture to seize pirates and prey upon French shipping, became worried. They sent a spate of letters to ports of the West Indies, hoping to trace the *Charles* and recover their investment. No response came. The ship was not in the West Indies. By November the *Charles* was in the South Atlantic.

Heading for the waters of Brazil, Captain John Quelch, with considerable guidance from quartermaster Holding, began a career of piracy and murder that would make him notorious. Holding always stayed in the background, letting Quelch have the glory. In the next three months he captured nine vessels—five brigantines; a 12-gun ship of about 200 tons carrying hides and tallow and manned by a crew of 35; a small shallop; and two fishing boats. Unfortunately, these vessels did not belong to Britain's enemies, the French, but instead to the king of Portugal—an ally. Portugal owned gold mines and the French did not, which undoubtedly accounts for the ships' being seized. On May 16, 1703, Great Britain and Portugal had signed a treaty at Lisbon. Certainly the captured Portuguese ships were aware of this alliance.

The crew's booty was incredibly rich! A later account of it enumerates a hundred weight of gold dust, coins valued at over 1,000 pounds, ammunition, small arms, fine fabrics, rum and provisions.

In May of the following year Quelch and his crew returned to Boston, and as they entered the harbor the captain thought of his last act on their departure.

"Do you remember the coin I threw for luck at Halfway Rock?" he asked Holding as they stood at the rail of the *Charles* and passed the familiar landmarks. "It worked."

"Oh, yes. It worked," said Holding, smiling faintly. To Quelch's disappointment, Holding refused his invitation to go drink to their return. Seemingly in a hurry, he disappeared into the throng of seamen going ashore as soon as the ship was anchored in Marblehead Harbor. The rest of the crew began to scatter, heading for Salem, Cape Ann and villages in Rhode Island.

On shore in every tavern and bawdyhouse John Quelch boasted of his luck. He claimed to have come upon a wreck in the West Indies and to have recovered from it a great treasure. There was much talk. Taverns and stores of the fishing villages told of men from Quelch's crew carelessly measuring gold dust, flinging down coins and gold bars with no idea of the value. Such wealth had never been seen before. As word of the riches spread, tongues began to wag skeptically about the captain's story.

Ship owners and merchants who followed the movements of seagoing vessels began gossiping in the pubs once more, recalling the sudden disappearance of the *Charles* the previous summer and speculating about its reappearance.

An item appeared in the Boston *News-Letter*, a brand new publication in its fifth edition:

> Arrived at Marblehead, Capt. Quelch in the Brigan-
> tine *Charles* that Capt. Plowman went out in, are said to
> come from New-Spain & have made a good Voyage. May
> 15-22, 1704.

The *Charles'* investors, unaware of their vessel's return, read this with surprise. The governor was temporarily absent, so Attorney General Paul Dudley, son of the governor, immediately set out in pursuit of Quelch and his crew. The next day a proclamation was issued by the lieutenant governor announcing that John Quelch and his men had "lately imported a considerable quantity of gold dust, and some bar and coined gold which they are violently suspected to have gotten and obtained by felony and piracy from some of her Majesties friends and allies and have imported and shared the same among themselves." The announcement noted that there had been no judgment from the authorities that this was a lawful prize.

Quelch's name was on everyone's lips. Officers of the law were commanded to capture captain and crew and hold any treasure they possessed. Within two days, Paul Dudley had Quelch and six of his men in the Boston jail, three in jail at Marblehead, one (a James Austin) held at Portsmouth and another in jail at Salem; one other was being delivered from town to town by each community's constable. The search continued.

When Governor Joseph Dudley returned from his trip to settle a minor legal matter, he was not satisfied with the proclamation issued by his lieutenant governor. He issued another saying that the gold and treasure had been taken from subjects of the king of Portugal and naming murders that John Quelch and his crew had committed. The pirates caught were in possession of 49 ounces of gold dust.

Matthew Pymer and John Clifford, two New Englanders who had been forced, would become witnesses for the queen. They talked long before the trial, and their testimony would hurt Quelch, for they described his refusal to put them ashore at their request and his "piratically taking various vessels belonging to subjects of the King of Portugal, Her Majesty's good Allie." They told of the capture of the 200-ton ship, of how Quelch's men had murdered the captain and wounded some of the Portuguese crew.

Pymer and Clifford testified that Plowman's cabin door was nailed closed with a marlin spike on the orders of the ringleader, Anthony Holding, who plotted with the crew to seize the *Charles*. When John Quelch came on board he made no protest to holding the captain prisoner in his cabin nor to the plot to take over the ship. These "Matters of Fact" were determined in a hearing held in the first week of June, and on the morning of June 9, 1704, Quelch was escorted to the courtroom where he would be tried for his life.

The charge was that as lieutenant commander of the brigantine *Charles*, he had disobeyed his ship's owners and had refused to set ashore Matthew Pymer and John Clifford, who "dreading your Pyratical Intention, earnestly desired the same." Holding Pymer and Clifford against their will, Quelch had set his course for the Brazilian coast, where he had begun to capture Portuguese vessels.

It was clear at the trial that Holding was the ringleader, but Captain Quelch did not protest. Anthony Holding was never found, and it is said that he escaped to Snake Island, where he buried 320 ounces of gold dust. He was later lost at sea. The gold retrieved from Quelch's treasure, tilting the scales at almost 800 ounces, was sent to England.

Along with Captain John Quelch, John Lambert, Christopher Scudamore, John Miller, Erasmus Peterson, Peter Roach and Francis King were tried and sentenced to death. Where were they from, these men who turned to piracy? Captain John Quelch was born in London, Lambert in Salem, Massachusetts; Scudamore had been apprenticed to a cooper in Bristol, England; Miller came from Yorkshire; Peterson was a Swede, Roach an Irishman and King was born in Scotland.

John Lambert was probably typical of many New Englanders who became pirates. He was married, had children and was about 49 years old at the time he was caught and executed. His parents and grandparents were poor fishermen, and to him the rewards of piracy, as promised by men like Holding and Quelch, must have exceeded his wildest dreams.

He testified that when the captain was shut in his cabin he was sick in the gun room and was forced to go on the voyage south. But his fellow crew members testified that Lambert was as active as all the rest and never refused his share of the spoils. In reply Lambert maintained that if he had not accepted spoils he would have been killed or marooned. He was convicted.

It was on Captain Quelch that Puritan minister Cotton Mather expended his greatest effort, trying to cause him to repent. "Faithful Warnings to prevent Fearful Judgements" was his sermon on the day of the pirates' execution. Mather walked in solemn procession to

Scarlet Wharf, continuing by water to the gallows set up off a point of land below Copp's Hill (where the North End Park bathing beach would someday be). According to the grisly custom of the day, the bodies were to hang on display until only the skeletons remained. Only Lambert escaped this fate. His son and widow petitioned to have his body turned over to them, and they buried it in the family graveyard that night at midnight.

Despite the best efforts of Cotton Mather, Quelch did not repent, and his gallows speech was cynical.

"Take care how you bring money into New England, to be hanged for it!" he warned and then complained, "I am condemned only upon circumstances."

In his death agonies perhaps Captain Quelch thought bitterly about how Holding had duped him. Alive and rich and free—at least for the moment—the man who had led him down the path of piracy had used him to carry out his plan from the start.

William Fly
American Coast to West Indies

C aptain James Green was ready to leave Jamaica when he found his longtime boatswain missing. It was an April afternoon in 1726, and Green's vessel, the *Elizabeth* of Bristol, England, was to sail for the coast of Guinea. Boatswain George Tolliver had been one of his favorite crewmen, and Green was puzzled by his sudden disappearance. He must replace him as soon as possible—not such an easy matter at the last minute—and somehow the problem gave him the feeling that the voyage was ill-starred.

Quartermaster Alexander Mitchel, who had drawn his attention to Tolliver's absence, spoke up.

"Sir, may I recommend an experienced man eager to ship out with us? I'll wager he's good as Tolliver."

"And who may the fellow be?" Captain Green asked.

"Fly. William Fly. I asked him to come aboard, sir, beggin' your pardon for bein' so bold. But you can see what you think about him."

Still trying to shake his feeling of unease, Green hesitated; then relief at having his problem solved won out. "Fine," he said.

A tall, heavy-set man stepped forward.

"Captain Green, this is William Fly."

His hair was sparse, his beard a grizzled pepper and salt. The tanned skin stretched taut over his thin face had the texture of leather, and the way his eyes caught the light gave them a fierce animal look. Again doubt welled up within Green, but due to the lack of time before they sailed he forced himself to ignore his first impression. Though he was always one to heed his intuition about men, just this once he chose not to. He heard himself say, "Glad to have you aboard," and he gave his new boatswain a smile.

The *Elizabeth* sailed out of Jamaica on schedule at daybreak. For the first week all went well. Then the captain, with that strange sense of dread, noticed that Fly was becoming thick with some of his more unsavory crew members—among them Samuel Cole, Henry Hill and Thomas Winthrop. Alexander Mitchel, too, was often with them.

It was a night when the moon was there one moment and gone the next, and when the stars were hidden by the clouds, that Fly revealed his plan. The tones of his voice were hoarse and low so the men around him had to lean forward and strain to hear.

"Some say I've been a pirate. I'll tell you right off, it's God's truth. Does that bother you?" The men snickered, so Fly went on. "I sincerely hope not, gentlemen, for I know how to make us all rich."

"What are you talking about?" asked Mitchel, who well knew what it was.

"I'm talking about doing away with the captain and mate, and voting William Fly your captain, men." His voice became conspiratorial. "And then together we'll make the *Elizabeth* a real pirate ship."

There was a shocked silence, then an excited murmur of voices, and suddenly a rousing vote of approval. It was May 27—a little over a month since the ship had sailed.

That night, with Fly in the lead, Mitchel, Hill, Cole and Winthrop quietly slipped up behind helmsman Morrice Cundon, who had the one o'clock watch. At the last minute he heard them, spun around and gaped in frightened surprise.

Before Cundon could open his mouth, Fly said, "If you speak one word or stir either hand or foot, I'll blow your brains out."

And another of them said, "We'll see that he goes into the drink to join Tolliver, that pious boatswain!"

They tied Cundon with his own shirt, and one of them took his place at the helm. Then Fly, cutlass in hand, and Mitchel accompanying him, slipped quietly to the captain's cabin. They were cautious, not knowing if they had waked him and whether he had reached for a pistol. He was asleep. Seizing the captain's shoulders, they shook him roughly.

"What's wrong?" mumbled Green.

"We've no time to answer stupid questions," replied Mitchel. "It will save us the time of scraping you up from the deck if you'll come quietly."

"This is no way to treat your captain," exploded Green, now wide awake.

"I'm the new captain, not you," said Fly. "We can't waste provisions feeding useless men—men like Tolliver."

Captain Green knew then with a shock that his first doubts about Fly had been correct. But the knowledge came too late. The crew had mutinied, and his own life was in danger.

"I've never been harsh with either of you, so you certainly have no reason to kill me out of revenge. If it's your security you're thinking about and won't take my word that I shan't obstruct your plan, put me in irons until you can set me ashore."

"And let you live to hang us!" said Fly. "Oh, no. We can't take that promise. It's hanged many an honest fellow already."

Mitchel and Fly seized Captain Green and pulled him from his bunk.

Entreating them to spare his life for his soul's sake, the captain said he would take a solemn oath never to testify against them and pleaded to be allowed to live a little longer.

"I am not fit to appear in judgment before a just and pure God. I am loaded with sins," said he, begging them not to send him to his death and doom him to punishment forever before he had time to cleanse his soul with the tears of repentance. "If you believe that I'm a threat to your future safety, at least give me time to prepare for death, just as the law would give you should you later be taken."

"No preaching," said Mitchel. "Be damned if you will. What's all that to us?"

The captain stumbled, then fell on his knees, but they forced him to rise.

"Get up and go on deck, you dog, so we shall lose no more time with you," growled Fly impatiently.

They dragged him through the steerage and up to the deck.

"Would you rather take a leap like a brave fellow or be tossed over like a sneaking rascal?" asked one of the conspirators with an evil smile.

Turning to Fly, the captain pleaded with his former boatswain. "For God's sake, don't throw me overboard, for if you do I'm forever lost; Hell's the payment for my crimes."

"Here's what we'll do for this poor soul," shouted Fly to his men. "Since he's so godly we'll give him time to say his prayers, and I'll be the preacher."

The captain looked appalled, but Fly continued in a sardonic voice.

"Repeat after me. *Lord have mercy upon me.* Short prayers are best so no more words, Green. Now over the side with him, my lads!"

The captain continued to beg for mercy. "Only an hour—give me just one hour."

But his pleas were in vain. With the captain still crying out piteously, the conspirators seized him and heaved him over the rail. His frantic movements made it difficult for them to throw him far from the boat, and just over the side he managed to catch and hang on with one hand to the mainsheet. Winthrop ran to get the barrel maker's broadaxe and with a swift, merciless blow he struck Captain Green's hand, severing it at the wrist. Green's body plummeted into the water below.

"Now for the first mate!" shouted Fly exuberantly.

Jenkins was brought up. He fell on his knees on the deck, pleading for his life. But the new captain had already shown he was not a man who understood the meaning of compassion.

"You eat in the captain's mess, and the pair of you should drink together," jeered Fly.

"Yes," joked the crew, "it's a pity to part good company."

They made fun of him in his agonies and, seizing his hands and feet, began to swing him back and forth. When his body had the momentum to clear the ship, oblivious to his screams, they tossed Jenkins over the rail.

Off the coast of Carolina, Fly seized several ships, one belonging to a Captain Fuller. For no apparent reason, Fly ordered Fuller stripped and cruelly lashed. Fuller's ship had grounded upon one of the many shoals in the area and the pirates attempted to burn her, but she bilged, and however hard they tried, they could not get even the part of her above water to burn. They left her to sink. Captain Fuller and his crew asked to be put ashore, but Fly refused, saying he would release them the first vessel he took. It was an empty promise.

On June 5, 1726, Captain Fly set sail from Carolina, and next day the *John and Betty*, commanded by a Captain Gale, crossed their path. Gale was heading for Guinea.

Fly immediately gave chase. Unable to catch the ship, he sent up a signal of distress, hoisting his jack at the main-top-mast head, but this did not deceive Captain Gale. All night Fly pursued him. Finally the wind slackened, and he was within shot of the ship. Hoisting the black flag, he fired several guns and drew close to board the vessel. Gale, poorly armed, struck his flag and surrendered. Then Fly and his crew, brandishing pistols and cutlasses, boarded their prize. Tying Gale hand and foot and sending him as a prisoner over to Fly's vessel, they fanned out to search the *John and Betty* but found nothing other than sailcloth and a few pistols. There was no celebrating that night, for Fly and his men were angry over the lack of booty. The ship was worthless to them, and in two days they let her go, but not before taking off six of Gale's best men and forcing them to join the pirate crew.

Captain Fly decided they would find more vessels and more ports to sell their plundered cargo farther north, along the New England coast, rather than in Carolina and Virginia. He evaluated the number of men in his crew. They still held Captain Fuller as a passenger and also Captain Green's surgeon. But to Fly the most important man was a Captain Atkinson, recent master of a ship they had taken off Carolina. He was an excellent pilot and Fly believed he knew the coast of New England well. Fly's crew liked the fact that he was a gifted artist whose entertaining sketches could help them while away the long hours at sea. Fly freed the other prisoners, but when Atkinson asked to go, too, Fly burst into a blood-curdling stream of oaths, ending with a threat: "Understand me, you fool of a captain. You will stay to act as our pilot, and if you plot the wrong course, I'll kill you."

"It's unwise for me to risk everyone's life, since I don't know the coast," maintained Atkinson. "Nor is it fair that one mistake made in ignorance should cause me to lose my own life. I beg you, put me aboard the smaller boat with Captain Gale and let me go."

"No! Stop that palavering. It won't save your bacon," Fly said furiously. "Either discharge your trust as an honest man or I'll send you to the devil. No more words about the matter."

Atkinson held his tongue and set the course for New England. When they were off Delaware Bay they met a sloop, and Fly immediately gave chase. Coming alongside her, Fly hoisted the black flag and ordered the sloop to strike her colors. She hurriedly did so, and the captain sent Atkinson aboard to sail her, but would not allow him any arms.

The sloop was commanded by a Captain Harris, and when they boarded the pirates found 50 frightened passengers but no booty. Again they had gone to the trouble of chasing and seizing a prize to find themselves no richer. Keeping only a sturdy young man named James Benbrooke, they let the sloop go.

Back on Fly's ship the captain ordered Atkinson to bring the *Elizabeth* into Martha's Vineyard harbor. Atkinson missed the place. Before he realized what was happening, the captain saw a landmark that told him he was already beyond Nantucket. He was sure Atkinson had tricked him.

"You rascally scoundrel!" he shouted, striking the pilot about the head. "It was a piece of cruelty to let a villain such as you live, who intends the death of so many honest men."

"Sir, I never pretended to know the coast. It is hard to die for being thought an abler man than I am or ever made myself out to be. Am I to suffer for your misjudgment?"

"You abominable villain! Your plan is to hang us," bellowed Fly. "Blood and wounds! You won't live to see such a sight, you dog!"

Fly ran toward his cabin and returned with a pistol, but Mitchel, who believed Atkinson was innocent, stopped him from shooting.

Now Atkinson, who was in truth a clever fellow who had never ceased planning his escape, saw how narrowly he had escaped death with his feigned accident of navigation. He settled on a new plan. He would make friends with the pirates. He led them to believe—not by any promises, but by words he dropped casually—that he was considering joining them. And always he entertained them, watching the men as they worked and giving them sketches of themselves. He became so popular that there were even hints among the crew that Atkinson would make a fine substitute for the hot-tempered Captain Fly. He did not encourage this talk, but he continued to leave the pirates with the impression that he would join their numbers. In return they protected him from Fly, who thought Atkinson would betray them at the first opportunity and often suggested throwing him to the sharks. Gradually, pressured by his men, Captain Fly changed his tune and began to place more and more trust in Atkinson.

The navigator had insinuated himself into a position of some favor with Captain Fly by the time they met a fishing schooner east of Nantucket. Firing a gun and hoisting his black flag, Fly came up beside the schooner, and Atkinson was close enough to see the crew's terrified faces.

"Bring to and put your boat with your captain in it on my ship, or I'll bloody well sink you!" swore Captain Fly.

The schooner captain hurriedly complied. When he arrived, Fly began to question him as to the kind of vessels he would meet as he proceeded north.

"If you can give me information about a good sailing ship in my path, it would be to your advantage; otherwise I shall just keep you."

The terrified captain was more than willing to sacrifice someone else's ship if he could win his own release.

"I have a companion vessel on this trip much finer and better suited to your needs than mine, and it will soon be in sight."

About noon of the same day the promised companion hove into view. Sailing the captured schooner to avoid suspicion, Fly manned her with six pirates along with a prisoner named George Tasker and sent her in chase. On his own ship Captain Fly had kept only three pirates, Atkinson and 15 forced men. Atkinson was quick to note that the pirates were outnumbered more than five to one, but Fly had not forgotten to keep his arms beside him on deck.

Atkinson spoke quietly with Benbrooke and a seaman named Walker. "Be alert," he said. "We may have a chance for freedom."

They had just settled upon a signal to seize the captain when, as if by an act of providence, several fishing vessels appeared on the horizon.

"Captain! I see some prizes ahead." Atkinson shouted. "Come here and let's see if we can make them out."

Bringing his binoculars, Fly walked toward him. Atkinson saw the captain had left his firearms on the quarterdeck, and he gave the prearranged signal, but no one moved. The captain was now only a few yards away. Suddenly, to Atkinson's vast relief, the two other seamen sprang upon Fly, pinning his arms behind his back. A stream of oaths more foul than any Atkinson had yet heard poured from the captain's mouth. But it was clear they had him, and Fly then lapsed into a sullen silence.

Atkinson brought the vessel—pirates, prisoners, forced men and all—into Great Brewster, where a guard was placed aboard. When the pirates were brought to trial at the courthouse in Boston, Atkinson testified against the captain. Only once did Fly look at him—hatred burning in his eyes like the fires of hell. He and three of the pirates were condemned and the execution set for July 12.

Atkinson recalled Fly's words to him after he had deliberately missed putting in at Martha's Vineyard.

Your plan is to hang us! Blood and wounds! You won't live to see such a sight, you dog!

On the last count the captain had been wrong.

Near the entrance to Boston harbor, Atkinson saw William Fly one more time. It was after the execution. Shipping out as navigator on a fine, fast sailer, he glimpsed, silhouetted against the blue of the sky, the body of Captain Fly hanging in chains.

Charles Gibbs
New England

D uring his early years Charles displayed a quick mind, a bad attitude and a determination to break the school rules. The schoolmaster had told his father angrily, "That boy's a young devil."

Not surprisingly, such qualities resulted in expulsion. Put to work on the family farm, Charles Gibbs was refractory and headstrong. In spite of all this, when the elder Gibbs discovered that his eighteen-year-old son had disappeared while accompanying him to Providence for the day, he was ashamed at his own sense of relief.

Later he learned that Charles had run away to sea, shipping out on the sloop-of-war *Hornet*. Hearing news that their son had distinguished himself in action against the British, the Gibbses felt a sense of pride in Charles. It was one of the few times since his birth in 1794 that he had ever made them proud.

After the war was over Charles told his parents he was going into the grocery business and settled in Boston. Obtaining financing from friends, he opened not a grocery but a groggery called the "Tin Pot," on Ann Street—characterized by many as a "place of abandoned women and dissolute fellows." Charles's ability to consume liquor surpassed his business talent; the store failed, and soon he was back at sea.

It was while he was on board a privateer out of Buenos Aires that he became a pirate—"a devil of a man," some would later call him.

Charles Gibbs's career began when a quarrel developed between the crew and the officers of the ship about how some prize money should be divided, and it led to mutiny. The mutineers selected Gibbs as their captain. Putting the officers off the ship on the Florida coast and leaving them to find their way to the nearest settlement, Gibbs set course for the West Indies. It was a highly successful voyage, for en route they seized 20 vessels.

While many pirate chieftains set men from a captured ship adrift in a small boat or left them on islands where they stood a chance of being rescued, Gibbs did no such thing. He ordered his men to slaughter the crews in cold blood, and it was later estimated that he killed well over 400 people. Word of his infamies spread—probably from talk among his own crew when they were in various ports. But Charles Gibbs was not easy to capture.

In Havana he boasted to his comrades of staying at the same lodgings as officers from the United States and overhearing their plans to capture him before he left harbor. Cuban officials were no help to the frustrated American officers seeking Gibbs. The officials knew the cargo he brought in was stolen goods, but it was so profitable to Cuban trade that they looked the other way.

Charles Gibbs, staring through his binoculars, could tell from the way the distant ship rode in the water that it was heavily laden, and his eyes shone with excitement. As it drew closer he judged it to be one of the newest and finest in the Indies fleet. The dark, bead-like rim above the rail became the heads of passengers gathered to watch the approach of his vessel. He smiled and lifted his glasses again, sweeping them the length of the ship, searching for mounted guns and satisfying himself that there were none. This would be easy prey.

The ship belonged to the Dutch East India Company, and like most of the vessels returning from a foreign port, it was magnificently decorated, with the bright red lion-of-Holland figurehead baring its teeth at the sea. The scrolled and carved hull was painted a handsome green and gold, and above it all the ship displayed a towering spread of white sail.

At the sound of Gibbs's guns, the Dutch vessel surrendered. Gibbs and his crew slaughtered everyone on board with the exception of a beautiful young girl named Annekin. For the first time in his life the pirate seemed taken with one of his victims, although it did not keep him from brutally murdering her parents and fiancé before her eyes. Gibbs took the girl to the western end of Cuba, and there he and the other pirates abused her for two months. At the end of that time they were ready to move on and could not decide what to do with her, so they began to discuss her fate.

She pleaded piteously with Gibbs for her life. "Just leave me here or put me off anywhere," she begged, but the pirates' consensus was that for their own safety she must die. The question was how, and Gibbs decreed poison. After the degradation to which he had subjected her and the gory death of her parents and fellow passengers, she must have thought that a kindness. Annekin's trembling hands accepted the cup, and she drank it quickly. Gibbs and his crew went on their way.

His career in Havana waters continued. Then, while he and a confederate were plundering a ship they had just captured, a British ship interrupted them on the scene. The sloop-of-war fired, and Gibbs ordered his men to land and erect a four-gun battery to hold off the attack. Unable to hold the beach, they abandoned their vessel, destroyed everything they couldn't use and fled.

The British, landing almost on their heels, explored the secluded natural harbor and were shocked to find a dozen burned vessels surrounded by the most gruesome human remains. Gibbs had followed his usual practice of ordering his crew to murder all witnesses to their crimes.

Pursued, the pirates' only escape route was slogging through rough country on foot, each carrying his share of the booty. Gibbs made it over the mountains and reached Havana. He did not pause to enjoy his usual amusements of drinking and gambling, but with 30,000 dollars in his pocket, he set out for New York and Boston. After squandering money in both cities, he made a brief visit to Liverpool, satisfying a whim to go to England, and returned to New York only when his money was gone.

Enlisting in the war between Brazil and the Republic of Buenos Aires, he sailed from Boston on a ship called the *Twenty-fifth of May* to defend the Republic. Gibbs, rascal that he was, always presented himself well, and he had been commissioned a lieutenant. He often made this good impression just long enough to instill hope in his long-suffering parents or gain the confidence of his military superiors.

Admiral Brown respected his ability to such a degree that he placed him in command of a privateer mounting two long 24-pound guns. He made two good cruises before he was captured by a Brazilian cruiser and recognized as having been in the service of the enemy. They promptly jailed him in Rio de Janeiro.

After his release the former privateer commander was convinced his fighting skills could be turned to more profitable pursuits, and he tried to offer his services to the Dey of Algiers, the Mohammedan tyrant and robber who was at war with France. Frustrated by the French in a bold attempt to reach Algiers, Gibbs headed back by way of Marseilles to Boston, where he booked passage to New Orleans. He wasn't there long when he met Captain William Thornby of the *Vineyard*, who was sufficiently impressed to sign him on his vessel bound from New Orleans for Philadelphia with a cargo of sugar, molasses and cotton. The *Vineyard* left New Orleans on a sunny day—a good omen for the voyage, thought the captain, and the winds could not have been kinder. But the ship would never reach Philadelphia.

Unfortunately for Captain Thornby, his ship was carrying more than sugar, molasses and cotton. It had not been more than a week at sea before word spread among some of the crew that there was

54,000 dollars in cash on the vessel.

Nine men were aboard—captain, mate, steward and six seamen, including Gibbs. With Gibbs as ringleader, three men—Thomas Wansley, the steward, Henry Atwell, and E. Church—began to hatch a plot to kill the captain and the mate and seize the money.

"What do we do with the rest of the crew? It would be devilish to kill them all," protested Church. Gibbs laughed.

On the first night Charles Gibbs and the three crewmen of the *Vineyard* planned to murder the captain, their plan fell through. Shortly before they were to carry it out one of them discovered a sailor who had overheard their plotting. His low, frightened moans of "I'll be the next to die" forced them to silence him with threats. They set another date—the night of November 22—but did not actually make all the necessary preparations, for despite Gibbs's urging, they still couldn't agree on whether to kill crewmen James Talbot and John Brownrigg. Both knew about their murderous plan but wouldn't join in, so Gibbs bolstered the resolve of Wansley, Atwell and Church to do it.

The conspirators struck the third night, two weeks from the date the ship had sailed. After midnight Atwell, a light in one hand and a knife in the other, stole up quietly behind the captain, dropped the light, seized the pump-brake and hit him a hard blow on the back of his neck.

"Murder! Murder!" shouted the captain desperately, but Gibbs seized his arms and ordered Wansley to grasp his feet. Ignoring his terrible cries, they swung him overboard into the sea.

Running upstairs from below to find out what had happened, the mate was struck over the head by Atwell and Church, who had expected him to emerge from the companionway. He staggered back down to the cabin, followed by Gibbs, who sought to find him in the darkness below but couldn't. Hurrying back up to the deck for a lantern, Gibbs shouted, "Follow me!" and the mutineers joined. With the lantern, they easily found the unfortunate mate, and Gibbs held his wrists behind him while the others struck him over the head. Then they dragged him up to the deck and swung him overboard. He did not drown quickly as had the captain, and twice he called from the sea, imploring them to save him.

The same frightened sailor who had disrupted their plans on the first night was now on his knees in the forecastle, praying. They thrust a mug of grog upon him and promised not to hurt him if he would help them with the boats. Then they began to search the vessel and found a keg of Mexican dollars. After dividing the property of the captain and mate—money, clothes and gold watches—each pirate had received about 5,000 dollars.

"How do we go about dividing the money in the keg?" asked Wansley.

"Divide it in heaps as near equal as we can make them," said Gibbs, who had taken command since the murder of the captain. And that was the way they did it—no one counting it out.

Brownrigg, Talbot and the third seaman who had refused to take part in the murders were forced to do all the work of sailing the vessel until they were some 15 miles from the Southampton Light. Here they got the boats out, put half the money in each and scuttled the brig, setting fire to her cabin. Taking to the boats, they made land about daylight. Gibbs, Wansley, Talbot and Brownrigg were in the longboat and the others in the jolly-boat. As they reached the sand bar just off the island, an accident happened: In the rough water the boats struck each other.

"Throw out the cargo—the money, too!" shouted Gibbs. Reluctantly the men in his boat dropped about half of the money overboard, but the crew of the jolly-boat was less wise. They wouldn't part with their share of the treasure, and the skiff was soon filling with water.

"Help!" they shouted. "Help, we're going to drown!" Gibbs and the other three in the longboat heard their cries but could only watch as their comrades went down. Gibbs, Wansley, and the two crewmen with them who had not joined in the murders were all that now survived of the crew. They managed to land on Barron Island off the coast of New York, and, with Wansley's help, Gibbs found a site and buried the treasure in silver coin they had been able to save. The weather was below freezing, and they knew they must find shelter quickly or die from exposure.

After searching the island for shelter until they were all weak from cold and exhaustion, Captain Gibbs found one house. It belonged to a man named Johnson—the only resident of this desolate place. Johnson did not like Gibbs's looks, but, aware of the knife tucked in his belt and moved by the imploring words of the others, he took the men in for the night. The innocent crewmen watched for their opportunity to talk with him, and it came while Gibbs and Wansley slept. They related the story of the mutiny.

Next morning, Johnson and the two innocent crewmen tied the wrists of Gibbs and Wansley and rowed them by boat to the mainland, where they were picked up by the police. Taken to New York, they were indicted and tried.

Visiting him in jail several times, Gibbs's father listened to his son's accounts of what he had done to the various ship masters and their passengers. It was obvious that the story of the lovely Dutch girl and her death was one of the few that weighed on Charles Gibbs's conscience, for he told it over and over.

In his confession, written at the end of his life, he says, "How often when the fumes of liquor have subsided have I thought of my good and affectionate parents, and of their Godlike advice! My friends advised me to behave myself like a man and promised me their assistance, but the demon still haunted me, and I spurned their advice."

Captain Gibbs and Wansley were found guilty of murder and piracy. Sentence was pronounced March ll, 1831, and when the judge addressed the prisoners, he was particularly scathing in his words to the Rhode Islander.

"Charles Gibbs, you had education and training that should have made you superior to the temptation of crimes such as this," he thundered. "Murder, robbery on the high seas, mutiny, scuttling and burning the vessel—for each there is the death penalty."

Hearing the sentence, Gibbs's father rubbed his lined forehead in a gesture of despair. The face of his son showed no expression.

According to law, the sentenced men's bodies were to be given for dissection to the College of Physicians and Surgeons. At noon on April 22, 1831, two ministers attended them to the execution place, and both Wansley and Gibbs professed sincere repentance.

Arranging the rope roughly about their necks, the executioner stooped down and picked up the hoods. Wansley's eyes rolled in his head and already seemed to bulge, while Charles Gibbs's lips worked hideously as if about to mouth some agonized protest. Then the executioner dropped the full black cap, like a last-act curtain, down to cover each man's horror-filled face. Beneath their feet the trap door of the scaffold fell. Jerking spasmodically, the two bodies writhed in the warm sunlight until at last they hung perfectly still. Thus died Charles Gibbs and his confederate.

Gibbs's father stood waiting until the crowd dispersed. The clothes Charles wore now, with their bold colors, were the ones he was wearing the morning he was captured. Gibbs, Sr. had taken them away and brought them back washed. Staring down at the limp form while the executioner lifted Charles's head and removed the noose from the broken, wobbly neck, the father thought of the family cemetery in the grove of trees behind the large white Rhode Island farmhouse. But they wouldn't give him the body to bury there. What was he to do now?

Suddenly his mind went back to that windy April day long ago when he was plowing a field. He could see the schoolmaster, walking toward him across the furrows of earth. He had stopped and waited for him. Then he had listened while the man announced angrily, "That young devil is expelled!"

The elder Gibbs mused sadly. As a father, where had he failed?

True to the schoolmaster's words in his youth, Charles had become *a devil of a man.*

Gibbs was born in 1794 near Providence, Rhode Island. He wrote a confession before he died on the scaffold in New York. Records of the United States Court of the Southern District of New York say that Gibbs's treasure—some 20,000 dollars in silver coin—was buried on the beach of Long Island a few miles from Southampton.

Rachel Wall
Massachusetts

"Rachel!"

She stirred.

"You heard me. Get up!" her mother called impatiently.

The girl stretched, delaying the moment as she did every morning. She finally obeyed, rising from the rough corn husk mattress and padding barefoot to the washstand, where she splashed water on her face from a tin pan. Sixteen-year-old Rachel Schmidt stood staring at herself, her blue eyes mirroring her discontent, and then she languidly descended the ladder into the kitchen.

Rotund from potato dumplings, sauerbraten and an assortment of homemade German sausages, her father was lowering himself ponderously into his chair at the table.

"What took you so long, Rachel?" Mrs. Schmidt asked.

"Reading my missal, mother," Rachel said virtuously.

"Your prayer book? That's a good girl." Mrs. Schmidt looked more cheerful, and Rachel helped her set out the breakfast of boiled coffee, eggs, scrapple and thick slices of homemade bread. In his deep, sonorous voice, her father intoned a lengthy blessing before he began silently dispatching his food. Her parents seldom talked to each other at the table, and Rachel, too, ate in silence, thinking that today would be like every other. When she had finished with the dishes, she could look forward to the chores—feeding the swine, gathering eggs—and in the afternoon there would be milk to churn until her right arm ached with the turning of the paddle. How she hated this farm. All farms!

Her parents thought that a visit to the dusty village of Carlisle, Pennsylvania, should be entertainment enough for anyone. They had no idea how Rachel disdained the drab storefronts, or that during every trip to town her only thought was, "Someday I'll get away from here!" The only thing she did like was watching the stupid farm boys gawk at her. Rachel Schmidt was a flirt. And she knew that she was very pretty, with her long, shining brown hair, fair skin, and eyes the color of bright blue sky.

Then came the letter bringing word of her grandfather's death. It was the first interruption the Schmidt family had ever known in the quiet routine of their life. Rachel had not been around old John Kirsch since she was a child, and she did not grieve for him; instead, she looked forward to the trip to Harrisburg with her mother as an exciting adventure.

On their arrival she was left much to herself while her mother sorted through clothing and decided what should be done with Grandfather Kirsch's furniture and the tools left from his lifelong work as a boatwright. Rachel spent most of her time down at the Susquehanna docks. She loved the swarm of activity, the shouts and curses of dock hands as they cautiously lowered the large crates from vessel to wharf. What a contrast to her quiet life at home!

The prospect of her grandfather's funeral didn't depress her in the least. In fact, she looked forward to attending so she could wear her beautiful new bonnet with bright blue ribbons. Mrs. Schmidt had planned to remove the unsuitable adornments and sew on black, but Rachel had thrown such a fit that her mother had given in. "Not the color a proper young lady should wear to a funeral" was the mother's disapproving remark, but the ribbons stayed.

After the service Rachel managed to give her mother the slip. It was mid-afternoon, and she set out for her favorite place—the world of the docks. Even before she reached the water's edge, the air assaulted her nostrils with the pungent odors of fish and fragrant spices, and her ears with the men's strident shouts.

Sauntering along near the ships at anchor, Rachel was enjoying the sailors' admiring glances when suddenly she was struck with such a blow between the shoulders that it knocked the breath out of her. The new bonnet went flying off her head.

A rowdy crowd of girls had passed, and one of them had jabbed her and taken her bonnet. Now they were tossing it from one to the other, screaming with laughter. A tall girl with dirty blonde hair grabbed it, jammed it down on her head and, with mincing steps, pranced back and forth close to Rachel.

"Look at me! Ain't I somethin' in my bonnet with the blue ribbons on it!" she said, tilting her head coyly from one side to the other.

Drawing her arm back, Rachel smacked the girl's cheek with all her strength, and as the blonde girl reeled, Rachel lunged for the hat. But the rest were upon her in an instant, pummeling and kicking and passing the bonnet from one to another to keep it maddeningly just out of reach. Rachel was giving them a real tussle, but there were too many.

"Can it, girls!" shouted a young sailor, wading into the melee. "Let her up!" He tried to recapture the bonnet, now dirty and torn.

"She your fancy girl friend?" jeered the blonde, holding out the battered, brimless piece of straw with one blue ribbon—all that was left. "Here, take it!" and she dropped it and ran. Rachel's face was purple with rage.

"I hate them!" Her fists were clenched, and tears streamed down her cheeks. "They ruined my new bonnet!"

The young man put his arm around her shoulders and began to comfort her. "I'm sorry, but it would probably have rained on your bonnet and ruined it anyway."

Rachel glared at him. "You some sort of weather prophet?"

He sniffed the air and looked at the sky. "Yep. Anyway, I'll get you a better bonnet."

"You will? You really will?" She thought about how the boys in Carlisle would stare at her if she had some real finery. "When do I get the bonnet?" she asked, gazing for the first time from the torn bonnet into the eyes of her hero—her rescuer.

"Soon as I have some money. What's your name?"

"Rachel."

"Mine's George. George Wall. Your hair's sure pretty with the sun shinin' on it that way."

Her face flushed with pleasure.

They had not talked long before the sun was covered by clouds, and in a few minutes there was a sudden downpour of rain. George guided Rachel under a shelter on the wharf, but she was already wet.

"See. I told you it would rain." The two sat close together protected by the roof.

"Is that your fishing boat?"

"Yep. We're here for repairs."

"For long?"

"If I have my way," he said, smiling down at her.

He wasn't at all bad looking, she decided. Of course, he was old, maybe even thirty, but he had tawny eyes with little sparks in them and black curls, and when he smiled she could see his straight white teeth. The sky cleared, and the rain was gone.

"Coming back tomorrow?" he asked.

"I might. If I'm not too busy," she said, giving him a sidelong look from under her lashes and hoping he would have the bonnet by then.

George's fishing schooner had a lengthy stay in port, and Rachel came to the docks every day. Sometimes she would walk for awhile as if watching other boats before she finally sat down on the edge of the dock near George and dangled a pair of attractive legs. Rachel Schmidt was muscular and strong from farm work, but still shapely.

"Tell me about your home port," she said one day.

"Boston? It's great. Something to do every minute. What's your port like?" he asked teasingly.

"It's a cowport! Just farms and a dull little town called Carlisle."

"You wouldn't want to leave it, would you?" he asked.

"Maybe."

"What do you mean, maybe?"

"Well, I've thought I might like to travel someday." She gazed enigmatically off into the distance. Then she said, "Time to go now or my mother will give me a raking over." She still hadn't received the gift of a better bonnet and thought maybe he had forgotten it. "See you tomorrow, maybe," she called back to him with a flirtatious smile.

Toward the end of his second week in port, George said, "Let's get married before I leave." He squeezed Rachel's hand hard, and her blue eyes filled with excitement.

"My mom would take on somethin' dreadful!"

"How are you ever going to travel? This place is only a village. Just wait 'til you see Boston," George bragged. "Now that's a real city!" He reached over and hugged her, and the other sailors hooted and whistled at them. Rachel was embarrassed. But the ring—a gold band with a small garnet—made her sure George loved her. "My dead ma's," he explained. He must really care about her to give her that, she thought.

"Ma, I'm engaged!" Rachel called out excitedly when she returned to her grandfather's house. She extended her hand to show her mother the ring. Mrs. Schmidt saw it with a swift intake of breath.

"Hmph! Probably brass and will turn! We know nothing about him," she protested.

"Well, I do, and you can meet him if you'll come down to the dock tomorrow."

"Rachel, now listen to me. The Schultz boys or Klaus Kurtz' sons—they're good farm stock. And that young widower, Gerhard Eisenhower. He really likes you, Rachel."

"But he's so quiet and dull, momma!"

"Hmph! Better a dull man than one who's too lively after you marry him."

"I haven't had anything lively in my whole life, mother!" Rachel cried out angrily.

Her mother's warning did not linger any longer in Rachel's mind than spring apple blossoms cling to the trees in a wind on Boston Commons. She liked George. True, she didn't like the way his friends acted, which often embarrassed her. They drank, caroused, and even kissed their girls in public. But George treated her differently—with more respect.

The ring made just the tiniest dark smudge on her finger, and George acted surprised. But he said right away that he would let her pick one out herself—along with a new bonnet—when he was paid from his next voyage.

On the last Sunday in April they were married in a small Catholic church near the waterfront. George pressed some money into the hand of the slightly shabby priest, who seemed in a hurry to get the ceremony over with. There were no wedding guests from home, and her mother had been too upset to come. In Carlisle folks would say these were bad omens for a marriage.

"It doesn't matter. You've got me," said George, his arm possessively encircling her waist, and Rachel was happy. She wouldn't be going back to Carlisle again anyway.

When the fishing schooner set sail for Boston, the river ahead was a path of flame, ignited by the morning sun. The voyage between the green banks and small towns, down the winding Susquehanna, through the reaches of Chesapeake Bay and up the coast to Boston, was their wedding trip. Rachel marveled at the sights.

In Boston, George took her to Nob Hill, where he made her knock on the door of the finest house she had ever seen. To her astonishment, they gave her a job as a maid then and there. Now she jingled more money in her pocket from one week's wages than her father earned in a month.

Each time George came home from a fishing voyage, he took

Rachel out at night with his drinking buddies and their rowdy female companions, and sometimes she was so tired she could hardly drag herself to work next day. "Leave that job and come to sea with me," George began to plead.

One night, George and his friends stayed out drinking too long, and the fishing schooner sailed without them.

"'Tis our good luck!" laughed George, who seemed without a care in the world. The rest of the crew were downcast.

"What do we do now?" asked a big fellow who had spent his money on ale.

"We'll be pirates and get rich, that's what!" George Wall shouted exuberantly, and at this the men brightened and emitted a chorus of raucous hurrahs. During the Revolution all of them had served on privateers, capturing British ships, plundering them, sinking one prize after another. They were told it was their patriotic duty.

"It will be like the old days!" exclaimed one.

But another shook his head. "Count me out, mates. It's a hanging crime these days."

Rachel heard him. "Is he right, George?"

"Well, it's a little different in peacetime, but we won't get caught," he said, tilting his wife's chin up playfully. "I promise. You'll live in the lap of luxury."

Rachel smiled.

"What about a ship?" someone asked dubiously.

"By tomorrow I'll have the biggest ship you've ever seen!"

And he did. George Wall convinced an invalid friend to let him borrow his idle fishing schooner—its loan to be repaid by half the price of "the catch." Rachel admired the way George always got what he wanted. Including her.

Rachel and George, along with the crew, had been at sea for a day or two when pirate captain Wall, sensing a storm was on the way, scudded into the secluded harbor at the Isles of Shoals, and there they rode out the gale. As the last gusts of wind subsided, the captain gave orders to set sail for the busy north-south route taken by the big shipping vessels.

Reaching it, he bewildered his crew by shouting, "Seize the sails, pull 'em loose, twist 'em. Make 'em look like they've been battered by the storm." Now the men understood. "Hoist the distress signal!" he ordered the first mate, then turned to his wife. "Rachel, pull a long skirt over those trousers. If a vessel heaves into view, wave your arms for help."

"Do we need help?"

"Listen to your husband, woman! We're the poor survivors of a disabled ship!" He gestured up at the sails hanging slack and twisted and laughed heartily as he winked at the mate.

Soon a trim vessel appeared on the horizon, and when it drew near, Rachel played her role admirably, with a little coaching. Gazing through his glasses, the captain of the New England ship, the *Plymouth*, saw Rachel and the torn sails, and he and his men "rescued" the grateful crew. Taking them on board his own ship, the *Plymouth*'s captain, a hospitable man, was not suspicious.

It was just before dawn and the men on the *Plymouth* were all bedded down and fast asleep when Captain Wall and his men rose stealthily. Before anyone could cry out, the sleeping crew lay in their own blood with their throats slit. For their kindness, the New Englanders had paid with their lives.

So quietly had the murderers gone about their work that Rachel slept through it all. When she did awaken, it was after sunrise, and she could hear men shouting. She found the deck awash with blood, and George and his crew tying weights to the bodies of the *Plymouth*'s crew. The new bride was horrified.

"George—they're all dead! Why didn't you just tie them up instead of killing them?"

Her husband put his arm about her waist a little drunkenly. "Sweetheart. What 'ja think being a pirate was all about?" He reached into the money chest, then grasped her hand and dropped several gold pieces into it. "Here," he said to mollify her. "And don't you forget, back in Boston we're goin' to buy a new ring, a new house and a pretty bonnet!"

Rachel had an idea.

"Their boat is bigger than ours. Let's take it," she suggested.

"How do you think the owners will think we got her? No. First, we'll transfer her cargo and the fishing gear to ours. Then sink her. When we sell the gear in port, we'll say we found her washed up on the Isles of Shoals after the storm—no survivors." Rachel looked at George Wall admiringly. Her husband was not only handsome but very clever.

The jubilant pirates drank the rest of the day until far into the night. They had a booty of 500 dollars in cash, and next day they sold the expensive fishing gear from the *Plymouth* in the port of Boston without exciting suspicion.

In July a savage hurricane struck the New England coast, and Captain Wall and his crew set out to sea in the storm's wake. This time they sighted a trading vessel, and again Rachel stood at the rail, waving her arms frantically for help. George Wall congratulated himself on having the wit to use these storms as a cover. He could play this game forever.

The ship, called the *Penobscot*, pulled alongside, and the captain hailed them with offers of help. Wall observed that the *Penobscot* had a crew of seven—a few more men than he'd counted upon, so rather than accepting their hospitable invitation to come aboard, he shouted to the captain that he thought it was his duty to stay with his ship and try to repair her. "We've got a bad leak in the hold, captain," he added. "Could you and your first mate give me a hand?"

The captain and the first mate boarded, and no sooner had they descended into the hold than Wall and one of his crewmen thrust a knife into each man's back. They had no time to cry out and died silently, dropping with a soft thud.

Rachel was frightened. "But what about the others still aboard?"

The number of the *Penobscot* crew had been reduced by two, but there were five more. Going above deck, George called across to the other vessel.

"Your captain says he wants some wedges, men. Can a couple of you fetch them over?"

Two sailors with wedges obligingly boarded Wall's schooner and went below. They would never hoist another sail.

Three seamen were left. Captain Wall and his crew abandoned all pretense now and with drawn pistols boarded the other ship. Two of the remaining crew members scrambled up the rigging, calling back frantic pleas to be put off in a boat. Wall shot one of them and the man's body plummeted down, bloodying the deck, while the other clung like an oversize fly to the rigging. Two of Wall's crew scurried up the ropes after him—dark spiders leaping upon their prey, piercing him with their daggers until his body dropped into the water.

The third and last man dashed down into the hold, and the crew followed. Rachel and George stood watching. Not yet 20, this last seaman was a nice looking, blue-eyed boy, and when he was found hiding below deck behind some barrels he was terrified. He immediately surrendered and, promising to serve with them, begged piteously for his life.

"Couldn't we use him, George?" pleaded Rachel.

"Shut up!" The glints in his eyes were fiery sparks, and he ran his dagger through the boy. Rachel shivered. She wondered why that one had had to die—he had looked about her own age. George Wall kicked the limp body to one side, mounted the ladder from the hold to the deck, with Rachel following him, and shouted to his crewmen. "Weight him down with a keg of caulking, and pitch him into the drink!"

At the rail, Rachel threw up. George seized her arm roughly. "Silly little fool! If he got drunk in port and talked, we'd all hang."

He left her and went down to search the hold. Tearing the lock off the captain's chest, Wall found a cardboard box inside it containing a sizeable sum of money. Although their profits didn't make them wealthy, the murders of several dozen people had at least produced a healthy income for the pirates—but as yet there was no bonnet for

Rachel. George promised part of the booty to his wife, and soon they were the picture of domestic bliss.

For awhile all went happily. George did have an uncanny sense of just the right moment when a storm had safely passed—the moment to set sail—and a talent for finding the right vessel to pounce upon and plunder. Then their luck ran out.

It was a summer day, and they were moored off the Isles of Shoals, taking advantage of their protection and waiting for an unusually violent storm to pass. The winds had been fierce, and today Wall expected to see more than one vessel that would be easy prey. When all was calm, he ordered his men to set sail.

His plan this time was to reverse the role, playing the part of the hero appearing from beyond the horizon to save the victims of whatever wrecked ship they might find. George chuckled as he told Rachel his plan and explained that he wouldn't need her at the rail this time.

"But you can help strip the bodies of valuables later. Mind you turn everything over to me. Everyone must get their share," he said.

"You don't object to my searching the latrine heads, do you?" Rachel asked. "I once discovered 30 pounds in gold wrapped in a black handkerchief in the captain's latrine."

Wall chuckled. "I remember."

"I was so quiet he and the first mate were still sound asleep when I finished searching," bragged Rachel.

"Because they were full of rum," he teased.

But in a few minutes he was serious. They had reached open sea, and suddenly, unexpectedly, the wind was rising fast. George Wall could not believe it. There was scarcely time to adjust the sails before gale winds returned with a vicious fury. What he had supposed to be the end of the storm was only the calm at the eye of a hurricane. Suddenly howling gusts of wind ripped at the sails, rain swept the deck in opaque sheets, and the fishing schooner plunged down into the trough between waves as high as masts on the tallest ships.

Terrified, Rachel curled within a heavy coil of rope. Rain pelted her face like sharp nails. She saw George and one of the crew hanging on to the rigging while an enormous black wave loomed over them. And then tons of water fell like a tumbling mountain and swept across the deck. All she could do was hold fast. As the wave receded she could feel the water's tug, and she thought its force would suck her into the maw of the sea. Then came a sound like the boom of a cannon, and she looked up to see the mizzenmast snapped in half—part of it hanging across the rail. Her husband still clung to the rigging, but the crewman beside him was gone. Another wave hung like a sea monster above them, ready to descend and tear at their fragile hold on life—tons of sheer, wet power.

Rachel's hand almost slipped as she felt the mighty weight of the water, and then the wave sucked at her body as if it would strip off the flesh. When the water retreated, she was so battered from objects that had swept over her that she felt dazed. She saw George and tried to shout to him. He looked like a limp sailor doll, holding on now with only one arm. Could she reach him? If she let go even for an instant she would be swept overboard.

Above the wind's roar she heard a loud crackling. The timbers of the cabin, struck by an advancing wave, had been torn from the deck. They surged over her husband, wresting his hand loose and sweeping him across the deck toward the rail. Then he was gone. She knew he was out there somewhere in the surging waves, tossing helplessly, carried this way and that. Had one of the timbers struck his head? Was he dead? If not, he was rapidly losing consciousness and the black water was already entombing him.

He was caught in that terrifying force he had always treated with such reckless familiarity, and in an uncontrollable fit of revenge it was crushing him in deadly embrace. For the first time, Rachel's husband had misread the weather, and it was his undoing.

She held on for her very life until she was stiff and sore, trembling almost uncontrollably before the wind. Then she managed to crawl into the hold, where she found the remaining crewmen. Two others besides her husband had been swept overboard in the hurricane.

Rachel took command of the ship. "Haul the braces tight! Move!" she shouted to the crew, and they obeyed without question. She must keep the rolling spars from having too much play. All that day the wind blew, and the sails began to work loose. "Lash the sails," she ordered. Sometimes the wind swept her words away. The ship was laboring. Water crashed to and fro upon the deck.

The wind blew all night and all the next day, on and on and on. But sometime during the night of the second day the wind subsided and the water became calm. Next morning they flung sand on the ship's planks and scrubbed off the green slime of the sea so that the deck was no longer slippery.

On the third day a brig appeared in the distance, and Rachel stood at the rail as she had so many times before. There was a trace of fog, and she waved the red shirt even harder than if it had been a clear day. As they watched hopefully, the brig's course changed, and it began heading away from them and out to sea. The two crewmen groaned in despair, for since they had left the Isles of Shoals they were out of water.

Another day passed, and with it more ships—all too distant to see the woman waving at the rail. Then a large vessel appeared to be heading in their direction, and again Rachel stood signaling frantically with the red shirt. Surely they would see her, if not the broken mizzenmast. The ship came toward them under full sail with what seemed every intention of coming to their rescue. Rachel waved desperately. Then the vessel veered. Hadn't the pilot seen them? She was so weak—so exhausted. Suddenly it resumed its course and came toward them. They were going to be rescued.

When the other vessel drew up beside them, its crew could see tears streaming down the woman's badly sunburned face—a pitiable sight. For the first time Rachel Wall's distress was real.

The ship dropped them off at Boston, where Rachel returned to her old employer, pleading a broken romance as the reason for her return.

She had decided to lead an honest life again. And all might have been well had it not been for one thing.

During her months at sea as a pirate, Rachel had acquired an insatiable appetite for luxury. There were valuables and money to be found on the ships anchored at the docks of Boston harbor, and for her, the danger of being caught enhanced the excitement. Searching the cabins—knowing the places where men hid money and valuables—had become second nature to Rachel while she and her husband pursued their careers of piracy.

One afternoon she was returning from the dock when she noticed a girl walking toward her. "Pretty but a real snob," thought Rachel, staring at her. What expensive clothes. That beautiful, fancy bonnet alone must have cost a fortune.

As they passed each other, Rachel Wall was seized with a sudden, overpowering urge. Reaching out, she struck the young woman to the ground with one blow and snatched the handsome bonnet off her head. While her victim lay stunned on the road, Rachel forced her fingers into the girl's mouth and tried to pull out her tongue! She heard footsteps approaching, and, jamming the girl's bonnet on her own head, she fled.

About 50 yards from the scene, Rachel heard the girl's scream. She must have recovered from her shock. Rachel looked over her shoulder, to see an officer giving chase. Frantically, she ran, clinging to the bonnet so it wouldn't fly off her head in the wind. If she had let it go, she might have been able to outrun her pursuer—her legs were as strong as ever—but she held on to the brim as if her life depended upon it. Then a strong arm seized hers, and she was arrested.

Rachel Wall was tried on the tenth day of September 1789, and the charge delivered to the jury was that "she feloniously did assault and take from the person of Margaret Bender, one bonnet of the value of seven shillings."

"I confess to having been a pirate," admitted Rachel boldly from the witness stand, "and I wouldn't mind being hanged for *piracy*, but to be tried for *robbery* is degrading!"

She protested her innocence to the last, but the verdict of the jury was that she be returned to jail and taken from there to the place of execution.

On the day of the hanging the maple trees encircling Boston Commons were unusually brilliant. A crowd gathered early, and spectators said that the girl would have been pretty had her face not appeared to be carved in granite. Rachel's expression was cold and impassive. When asked whether she had any last words to say, she looked contemptuously at the crowd and shook her head.

There was no appeal from a defense counsel, no public protest nor any request for a stay of execution from those who had followed the trial. In those days a person could be hanged for just stealing a bonnet. The jury had voted her guilty and the sentence was carried out. After Sheriff Joe Robinson had completed his grisly task, he sat down, and his awkward, unschooled fingers laboriously pushed the quill across the paper, forming the words, "Rachel Wall was hanged by the neck until she was dead."

And such was the fate of Massachusetts' famous woman pirate.

Seventeen-year-old Margaret Bender did not attend the hanging and never ceased to grieve over having been, as she saw it, the cause of the taking of a human life. Her beautiful bonnet had been returned to her, but she never wore it again. If she had known Rachel's past, or questioned the character of a woman who would try to pull out her tongue to prevent her from testifying about a stolen bonnet, the sentimental Miss Bender might have had fewer regrets.

Glossary

from *Falconer's Marine Dictionary* by William Falconer (1780).

bilge   That rounded part of the floor of the ship on either side of the keel that form[s] a transition between the bottom and the sides on the exterior of a hull. When a ship receives any damage or fracture in this area, she is said to be bilged.

bower anchor   One of the two side anchors of a ship.

bowsprit   A large boom or mast which projects over the stern to govern the fore part of a ship and counter force of [sails] behind it.

brigantine   A merchant ship with two masts. Not universally confined to vessels of a particular construction. Variously applied by mariners of different European nations.

broadside   Discharge of all the artillery on one side of a ship into the enemy at point blank range. *Or* "A squall of wind laid the ship on her broadside"—that is, pressed her down in the water, so as nearly to upset her.

canoe A sort of Indian boat or vessel formed of a hollowed trunk of a tree; sometimes of several pieces of bark fastened together. Largest, made of a cotton tree, may carry 20 to 30 hogsheads. Some made to carry sails (steeped in water to make pliant and extend sides). Strong beams placed across them to each side on which a deck may be placed. Can be sailed with sails of silk, grass or rushes. Most are rowed, not sailed.

careen Turn a ship on one side low enough in the water so that bottom is elevated and may be scraped clean of barnacles or filth.

club-haul To pull a single rope without assistance of block or tackle. [Or] Men dragging a seaman back and forth across a barnacle-encrusted bow as a painful form of punishment or abuse. [keel-haul]

come about Order to ship's crew to prepare for tacking.

companionway A staircase with a sort of wooden porch placed over the entrance; or the staircase of the master's cabin.

deck sloop A small vessel with a small covered deck suitable for lodging the men and also to preserve the cargo from the sea.

forecastle A short deck placed in the fore part of the ship above the upper deck.

frigate In the navy, a light, nimble ship built for sailing swiftly; mounted with from 20 to 38 guns. English were first with these and equipped them for war as well as commerce.

gunwales Upper edge of a ship's side.

hawser   A large rope halfway in size between a cable and tow line. Smaller than a cable; larger than a tow line.

jolly boat   May be a Danish yawl (jol). A light boat carried at the stern of a sailing vessel. Good in a high sea when a stout ship can hardly carry any sail.

jury-mast   A temporary or occasional mast erected on a ship to replace one carried away by a storm or broken in battle.

lie by   To arrange a ship by the side of another.

longboat   Largest and strongest boat belonging to any ship. Principally used to carry great burdens such as anchors, cables, ballasts, etc.

luff   Order from pilot to the steersman to put the helm towards the *lee* side of the ship, in order to make the ship sail nearer the direction of the wind (throw the ship's head into the wind in order to tack her).

mainmast   A name applied by sailors to whatever is principal, as opposed to secondary. This distinguishes the main mast, main keel, main hatchway, etc., from those that are secondary or inferior.

mainsail   One of the principal sails of a ship (such as the mainsail, foresail and mizzen). All sails are either three or four sided.

mainyard   Principal timber or longest of a ship. It is suspended from the masts of a ship to extend the sails to the wind.

mizzen   The aftermost of the fixed sails of a ship.

mizzenmast   The after mast upon which the topsails and stay sails are supported.

mizzen peak   The aft most of the fixed sails of a ship. Fore end reaches almost to deck. Aft end is *pecked* up above the middle of the yard (piece of timber) and there attached to the mast.

mizzen shroud   Aftermast ropes (shrouds) which extend from right to left side of ship, stabilizing the masts and enabling them to carry sails.

periagua   (or pirogues). A sort of large canoe used in Leeward Islands, South America, and Gulf of Mexico. Differs from "canoe" in that is is the trunk of **two** trees hollowed and united into one fabric.

pink   A name given to a ship with a very narrow stern. All vessels, however small, whose sterns are fashioned in this manner are called "pink-sterned."

poop   The highest and aftmost (behind and near stern) deck of a ship.

pump brake   A pump is used to discharge water from the bottom of a ship into the sea. The "brake" is the handle or lever by which the common ship pump is operated.

schooner   A small vessel with two masts.

shallop   A large boat with two masts and usually rigged like a schooner.

sloop   A small vessel furnished with one mast, the mainsail of which is attached to a gaff above, to the mast at its foremost edge, and to a long boom below.

sloop-of-war   A name given to the smallest vessels of war which are rigged either as ships or snows.

snow   A brig with a trisail mast set close to the main mast, on which a boom trisail is set.

tack   To change course (from starboard to port [larboard], for example) or to sail in a zigzag direction. This occurs by the arranging of the sails and force of wind acting upon them.

taffarel   The upper part of a ship's stern, being a curved piece of wood.

topsail   A large sail extended across the top masts by the top sail yard above, and by the yard attached to the lower mast beneath. . . .

topmast   The second division of a mast (the part between the upper and lower pieces).

wear around   To veer around. This is the opposite of tacking. A ship loses ground by this maneuver and it is rarely needed except when waiting for another ship or when wind and violent sea make tacking impractical.

yardarm   A long piece of timber suspended upon the masts of a ship to extend the sails to the wind. All yards are suspended either at right angles or obliquely.

Bibliography

Benton, Henry. *The History of the Pirates*. Hartford, Conn.: Henry Benton, 1834.

Brooke, Henry K. *Book of Pirates*. Philadelphia: J. P. Perry, 1841.

Carse, Robert. *The Age of Piracy*. New York: Holt, Rinehart & Winston, 1957.

Chatelain, Verne E. "The Defenses of Spanish Florida, 1565 to 1763." Carnegie Institution of Washington Publication 511. Washington, D.C.: Carnegie Institution, 1941.

Coffman, F. L. *1001 Lost, Buried or Sunken Treasures, Facts for Treasure Hunters*. New York: Thomas Nelson, 1957.

[Defoe, Daniel?] Johnson, Charles [pseud.?]. *A General History of the Robberies and Murders of the Most Notorious Pirates*. London: 1734.

Dow, George Francis, and Edmonds, John Henry. *The Pirates of the New England Coast 1630–1730*. Salem, Mass.: Marine Research Society, 1923.

French, Joseph Lewis. *The Great Days of Piracy in the West Indies*. New York: Tudor, 1961.

Gardner, Clifford L. *Black Caesar: Pirate*. Atlanta: Peachtree, 1980.

Gosse, Philip. *My Pirate Library*. 1926. Reprint. New York: Burt Franklin, 1970.

———. *The Pirates' Who's Who*. Boston: Charles E. Lauriat, 1924.

Hawes, Hildreth Gilman. *The Bellamy Treasure: The Pirates of the Whydah in the Gulf of Maine*. Augusta, Maine: Augusta Press, 1940.

Howell, T. B., comp. *A Complete Collection of State Trials and Proceedings for High Treason and Other Crimes and Misdemeanors from the Earliest Period to the Present Time, with Notes and Other Illustrations.* Vol. 15. A.D. 1710–1719. London: 1812.

Lee, Robert E. *Blackbeard the Pirate.* Winston-Salem, N.C.: John F. Blair, 1974.

Peterson, Mendel L. *The Funnel of Gold.* Toronto: Little, Brown, 1975.

Rankin, Hugh F. *Golden Age of Piracy.* New York: Holt, Rinehart & Winston, 1969.

———. *The Pirates of Colonial North Carolina.* Raleigh: North Carolina Department of Archives and History, 1963.

Ritchie, Robert C. *Captain Kidd and the War Against the Pirates.* Cambridge, Mass.: Harvard University Press, 1986.

Shomette, Donald. *Pirates on the Chesapeake.* Centreville, Md.: Tidewater, 1985.

Smith, Israel. *Mutiny and Murder, Confession of Charles Gibbs.* Providence, R. I.: 1831.

Snow, Edward Rowe. *Legends of the New England Coast.* New York: Dodd, Mead, 1957.

———. *Pirates and Buccaneers of the Atlantic Coast.* Boston: Yankee, 1944.

Stick, David. *Graveyard of the Atlantic.* Chapel Hill: University of North Carolina Press, 1958.

Trials of Stede Bonnet and Other Pirates. London: 1719.

Verrill, A. Hyatt. *Love Stories of Some Famous Pirates.* Glasgow: W. Collins.

———. *The Real Story of the Pirates.* New York: D. Appleton, 1923.

Whipple, Addison B. C. *Pirate Rascals of the Spanish Main.* New York: Doubleday, 1957.

Williams, Lloyd Haynes. *Pirates of Colonial Virginia.* Richmond, Va.: Dietz, 1937.

Wright, J. Leitch, Jr. "Andrew Ranson: Seventeenth Century Pirate?" *Florida Historical Quarterly* 39 (July 1960–April 1961).